Crossroads of the Eternal

Crossroads of the Eternal

M. Brett Callaway

RESOURCE *Publications* • Eugene, Oregon

CROSSROADS OF THE ETERNAL

Copyright © 2018 M. Brett Callaway. All rights reserved. Except for brief quotations in critical publications or reviews, no part of this book may be reproduced in any manner without prior written permission from the publisher. Write: Permissions, Wipf and Stock Publishers, 199 W. 8th Ave., Suite 3, Eugene, OR 97401.

Resource Publications
An Imprint of Wipf and Stock Publishers
199 W. 8th Ave., Suite 3
Eugene, OR 97401

www.wipfandstock.com

PAPERBACK ISBN: 978-1-5326-5382-7
HARDCOVER ISBN: 978-1-5326-5383-4
EBOOK ISBN: 978-1-5326-5384-1

Manufactured in the U.S.A.   NOVEMBER 5, 2018

Scripture quotations are from the ESV® Bible (The Holy Bible, English Standard Version®), copyright 2001 by Crossway, a publishing ministry of Good News Publishers. Used by permission. All rights reserved.

"If you believe that scientists are God-hating charlatans, this book may change your mind. Through heartrending real-life anecdotes, current events, biblical passages, and quotes from renowned scientists and theologians, Brett Callaway, a devout Christian and scientist himself, reveals that the true enemy in our battle is not science, but the adversary who fired the first shot with the words, 'Did God really say . . . ?"

—CHRIS YAVELOW, AUTHOR, SPEAKER, EDUCATOR

"In the tradition of his storytelling forefathers, Brett Callaway gracefully and easily tells the story of God's existence, his presence in this world, and how we are often blinded to the truth of this reality. And he does so in a refreshingly unassuming manner and in easy-to-read, straightforward language. We need more books like this!"

—KARL JOHNSON, DIRECTOR, C. S. LEWIS INSTITUTE, CHICAGO

"Dr. Callaway describes Godless 'postmodern, atheistic' processes men employ versus eternally beneficial processes where God and Christ have real authority. Crossroads of the Eternal is a dynamic place where all men live physically, emotionally, and spiritually, caught between the here and now and the timeless. Callaway astutely describes a yearning for the 'timeless' that is ingrained in all of us. This scholarly work offers excellent counsel regarding successfully satisfying that yearning."

—MATT BYERS, SENIOR ADVISOR AND EVANGELIST

"With a passion for lost souls Dr. Callaway has provided a jewel for saint and sinner. America has turned her heart away from not only her biblical heritage, but God himself. Dr. Callaway describes what has caused our spiral downward as a nation, and provides vital biblical solutions for our return back to God. As Joshua proclaimed he and his family's allegiance to God, so must America choose who we will serve."

—DON WESTRAY, PASTOR, LONGSTREET BAPTIST CHURCH, CUMMING, GEORGIA

Contents

List of Illustrations | *x*
Foreword | *xi*
Preface | *xiii*
Acknowledgements | *xvii*

1 God's Revelation: How God Shows Himself to Us | 1
   What is Revelation?
   General Revelation
   Special Revelation
   Study Questions

2 How Do We Know What We Know? | 11
   Sequence of Turning Information Into "Knowledge"
   Newness
   Evidence: Science, Faith, and Knowing
   Assumption
   Response
   Study Questions

3 Obedience | 22
   Turning From Obedience
   Turning to Obedience
   Following Christ
   Study Questions
   Westminster Shorter Catechism # 39

Contents

4 Authority | 34
   Our Problems With Authority
   Historical Examples of Authority in Society
   Authority of God in Our Personal Lives
   Discussion Questions

5 What Is Truth? | 44
   Conceptions and Outworking of Truth
   God Is Truth
   Discussion Questions

6 The Tyranny of Good Intentions | 54
   What Is Grace?
   Costly Grace
   Cheap Grace
   Despised Grace
   Exposing the Tyranny of Good Intentions
   Christian Life Under the Tyranny
   Setting the Captives Free
   Discussion Questions

7 Postmodernism and Power | 69
   The Hopelessness of Postmodernism
   The Will to Power
   Use of Crisis and Change to Overthrow and Transform
   Postmodernism and Destabilization of Society
   Enter the Crisis Phase
   The Final Solution: Normalization and the New World Order
   The One, True Hope
   Discussion Questions

Contents

8   Peace, Assurance, Boundaries, and Wonder | 82
    Senses
    Peace and Happiness
    Blessings of Boundaries and Wonder
    Faith in Christ: The Bond by which We Transcend to the Sacred
    Discussion Questions

9   Suffering | 93
    The Reality of Suffering
    Value and Purpose in Suffering
    Responses to Suffering
    Resignation
    Our Living Hope
    Discussion Questions
    Heidelberg Catechism
    Lord's Day 1: What is your only comfort in life and in death?
    Lord's Day 2: What must you know to live and die in the joy of this comfort?

10 Giving Thanks In All Things | 105
    Giving Thanks In All Things
    Unexpected Blessings
    Our Thanks and Our Lord's Example
    Discussion Questions

11 Crossroads of the Eternal | 115
    Human, Spirit and Our True Being
    Bound to the Timeless
    Life At the Crossroads of the Eternal
    Study Questions

Bibliography | 125
Subject Index | 129
Name Index | 132
Scripture Index | 134

List of Illustrations

Figure 1.1 Depiction of the Two Fundamental Metaphysical Worldviews | 3

Figure 1.2 Grace, or Higher Things vs. Nature, or Lower Things | 5

Figure 5.1 Circles of Living | 48

Figure 5.2 Fallacy of the Righteous Average | 51

Foreword

IN HIS BOOK *ESCAPE From Reason*, Francis Schaeffer said, "Every generation of Christians has this problem of learning how to speak meaningfully to its own age."[1] I grew up in the rural south where Christian language and imagery permeated the air—if not always the hearts. My Papa Callaway was a Baptist preacher. In fact, so many of the Callaways were Baptist preachers that a book was written about them.[2] My daddy was an agnostic, leaning atheist. I grew up listening to many religious and political debates between him and Papa while sitting in their living room.

On my mother's side, the Andersons were also Baptists who worshipped with a Pentecostal flair—when they went to church at all. I only recall them at church when someone died. But they were nevertheless very serious about their faith. It infused their lives, actions, and language. Papa Anderson had been a moonshiner, the son of the biggest (both by his size—he was called "Bigfoot" Anderson—and in volume of whisky sold) moonshiner in north Georgia. His younger brother Johnny died in his teens in Atlanta attempting to escape revenuers. Papa was a very gifted story teller, even for that generation of gifted story tellers who lived in the mountains of Appalachia and are now all but extinct—replaced by poseurs, mostly with leftist leanings who know nothing of the life mountain folks lived and who mock the God they loved. Although Papa had quit moonshining long before I was born, I grew

---

1. Schaeffer, *Escape from Reason*, 12.
2. Callaway, *Callaway Baptist Preachers*.

up hearing those stories and many others of life in the mountains in the early 1900s.

But today's generation is indifferent to even thinking about God; it doubts the existence of a spiritual world and doesn't believe in absolute truths, at least as a principle from which to discuss and resolve issues. In an ever-larger proportion of society, Christian traditions are not things to be clung to and treasured; they are despised as the causes of society's problems. Christians are often seen as foreign creatures speaking an unintelligible language, believing foolishness about God and spiritual things, and rigidly hindering progress through their bigoted stubbornness. The chasm between those brought up in the church and those outside the church is greater than at any time in our nation's history. This book is an attempt to begin to bridge that chasm. While I make liberal use of Scripture, I attempt to have it flow naturally from a context that doesn't require a Christian background or knowledge of the Bible.

Preface

SAM HAD CHANGED. HE was hardly recognizable. Years before, he seemingly had everything going for him. He was strong, handsome and rich, yet he was also grounded with the knowledge that he was the beneficiary of the hard work and sacrifice of his parents, grandparents, and great-grandparents. He also had an ever-present consciousness that his strength and riches were not the most important things. He was a religious man; he firmly believed his fortunate situation in life was due to God's favor, as a loving parent to his child, so he tried very hard to please his God by helping others. In fact, he was always very generous with his riches to those less fortunate, and quick to come to the rescue of those that were weak.

He wasn't perfect, but who is? However, he was exceptionally good—many said he was the greatest they ever knew. I suppose this partly explains where I saw him today. He had fallen so far! As is too often the case, others took advantage of his goodness and were envious of his greatness. It started in subtle ways. When he gave to those in need, instead of thankfulness, they began to say how much more they needed. He could afford to give more, they said. After a time, they even began to accuse him of being selfish. This struck Sam's tender heart. He began to doubt his motives. More troubling to Sam was how disappointing this would be to the God he loved like a father. He redoubled his generosity, then redoubled again. But the harder he tried and the more he gave, the more demanding and accusatory were those he gave to. As so often happens, self-doubts led to a downward spiral. He began to believe the terrible things that were said about him. He gave and gave, but instead of finding joy in it, he just felt guilty for not giving more—and his riches were running out!

Look at poor Sam today. He seems like a defeated man. He's consumed with guilt for having been strong and rich. He's almost neurotic with doubts about his motivations for the good he did—and still does. He is divided within himself. I fear for my Uncle Sam. I love him very much and want to see him more like his old self—healthy, strong, confident, rich, and still grounded in the knowledge that these are not the *most* important things. Many others would like to see him this way, too. Uncle Sam needs to regain his sense of purpose.

This, of course, is an allegory of America. How does an America that is ashamed of who she is, because she has forgotten who she was, find herself? How does she find herself and realign with the purpose she was made for? This phrase is laden with assumptions:

- "Made for" implies that we were made with intelligent intent. We aren't the result of randomness.
- "Made for a purpose" implies there is a "Purposer" with a plan and an ultimate objective towards which our purpose is aimed. It also implies that our lives and actions have greater meaning.
- "Aligning ourselves to our purpose" means that we are also aligned with our Purposer and that the Purposer will see his plan to completion.

These assumptions have been the underpinning of human belief and actions throughout the ages. Yet today they seem foreign. For almost two generations in America, and longer in other countries, these foundational beliefs have ceased to be taught. As a result, we have a fundamental inability to bridge worldviews—and this doesn't mean to reconcile them under a single, monolithic worldview, but merely to understand how a theistic worldview can be held by other human beings. Along with the loss of belief in God, or even gods and pagan spirits, there is an empty

Preface

self-centeredness whose only arbiter is power, and whose greatest motivating force is self.

This book is an attempt to speak to those who sense there is something very wrong with the belief—whether held consciously or unconsciously—that there is nothing other than the physical world, no powers beyond human and nature, and no purpose other than what we choose to create. The book is unabashedly Christian, but approaches worldly issues and Christian beliefs without assuming prior knowledge of Christianity. Those who have grown up in a Christian tradition will find this a bit backwards, but even for you, my hope is that this approach will cause you to think about your faith from a fresh perspective. If, on the other hand, Christianity is foreign to you, or you might even be hostile to it, this book is primarily directed to you. I grew up the son of atheist parents but had a Christian preacher as a grandparent. I loved and respected them all. From my earliest recollections I was exposed to debates on religion in general, and Christianity in particular, between my dad and his dad. I still have friends and family whose worldviews have tracked with society's, that is, from seeing Christianity as somewhat hypocritical a few years ago, to being militantly hostile to it today. In some ways I feel like Jacob, who wrestled with God at Peniel and told him, "I won't let you go until you bless me" (Gen 32:22–32). If you also wrestle with the questions of the world and how the world's answers about Christianity stand up to scrutiny, this book is for you. It is adapted from a Sunday school series I taught.

Not so long ago it was taken for granted that God exists. Today, there is a blindness to him even though he makes his presence known to all, so I begin by showing how better to recognize his presence and understand how he reveals himself to us. The next three chapters discuss how we move from an awareness of his presence to beginning to know him, and through a knowledge of him, begin to know what his purpose is for us and how our lives are shaped by that knowledge. Having seen how he reveals himself to us and how we know the world and see the world through different eyes, we look at how to apply our new view in the face of a society that remains blind to what we now see. Chapters five through seven explore truth first from the standpoint of its existence, then in how to recognize its counterfeits, and finally to understand the consequences of its loss. Chapters eight through ten look at how and why the ability to see God's hand in all aspects of life and to center our lives on him by faith in his Son Jesus Christ completely changes our lives for the better. Non-Christians often hear this claim made by evangelists. If these skeptics ask why the claim is true, too often the answer is in "Christian-speak" that is foreign to them. I attempt to bridge that gap and explain how Christians have found peace in times of suffering, even joy in the most horrific circumstances, enabling them to give thanks in *all* things.

In a sense, I finish where I started by looking at who we truly are, what kind of world this is, and how God has made all into his glorious plan.

Acknowledgements

THE DEGREE TO WHICH this book succeeds in its ambition is due in large part to the many helpful edits and suggestions given by my daughter, Jessie. It has also benefited from discussions with my wife Dorothy and my other daughter, Leah. The book would never have been started without the encouragement of many members of my Sunday school classes in North Carolina and my very dear congregation at Ira United Church in Ira, Iowa. Their questions and comments over the years have been challenging, stimulating, and always encouraging. Their striving to serve Christ in deed—as well as word—has been a light to my feet, as well as to my mind. I cannot thank them enough. And, finally I give thanks and all the glory to my Savior, Jesus Christ, who through all my shortcomings and excuses has opened door after door for this work to be accomplished, humble though it is. In spite of all the help I've had, it still has many failings. These are all mine.

1

God's Revelation
How God Shows Himself to Us

"The heavens above declare the glory of God, and the sky above proclaims his handiwork."

—PS 19:1

What is Revelation?

IMAGINE FOR A MOMENT that you go to a swimming pool, walk out on the diving board, and jump off. You go up or out and then down. Right? Repeat this ten times. What happens? Same thing. Repeat it one thousand times. What happens? Same thing. If you knew nothing about physics, what would you conclude? There is a natural law that "what goes up, must come down." Let's call it the law of falling. Now go to a swimming pool in a zero gravity enclosure and jump off the diving board. What happens? You continue in the direction you jumped. You realize that the "law of falling" is not a law at all. There is a greater underlying law that *controls* the law of falling. It's called the law of gravity. The presence *or absence* of gravity is what explains our experience. It is only when the normal (to us) condition of gravity is suspended that the wider set of possibilities to jumping off a diving board is revealed. In our ignorance of the existence of gravity, we would see our lack of falling from the zero gravity diving board as a miracle. You might say that a miracle is a window, or glimpse, of an as yet unrecognized law that controls what we experience as "normal." This is quite different from the commonly-held view of a miracle as being something that contradicts, or is at odds with, what we would consider to be "laws of nature." "Nature" is of course the natural world, the world we live in and that functions with a regularity we become accustomed to. It is "normal" to us. And that's the rub. Why should we have the conceit to believe what's normal to us is all there is? Before the discovery of gravity, the "natural law of falling" was all there was. Before the circumnavigation of the globe, the flatness of the earth was all there was. Before discovering the use of radio waves, having a voice coming out of a box would have been considered almost as miraculous as coming out of a burning bush. It isn't the closed-mindedness of religious people that limits the possibilities in life; it's the close-mindedness of those who believe what can be comprehended by the human mind is all there is. Fundamentally, there are two competing worldviews. One worldview believes all there is and all there ever will be, including God, belongs inside of the "box" of natural law. The other worldview believes that there is a reality beyond that which we will ever be able to fully grasp. In this worldview, God's reality lies outside of the box of natural law and even human understanding.[1]

---

1. Tackett, "Veritology, What is Truth?" Lesson 1.

Depiction of the Two Fundamental Metaphysical Worldviews

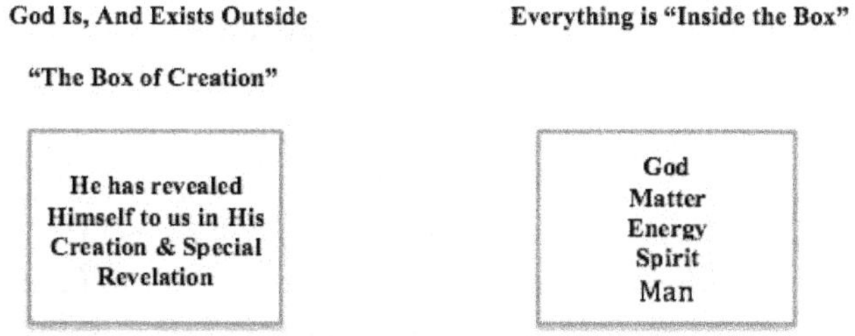

God Is, And Exists Outside

"The Box of Creation"

> He has revealed Himself to us in His Creation & Special Revelation

Everything is "Inside the Box"

> God
> Matter
> Energy
> Spirit
> Man

Figure 1.1 Depicts the two competing worldviews; one recognizes God as transcending creation and revealing himself through it, the other believes that everything including God, is contained within the "box" of the physical universe.

His reality is the "law," the fact that underlies and controls the natural world that we are accustomed to. What our minds comprehend is not a drop in the ocean of God's reality. God's reality is beyond our ability to even touch without his help. So he reveals himself to us. He does this in two ways, known as general revelation and special revelation.

General Revelation

General revelation is what God has revealed about himself to all through his creation, history and our conscience. It's what the apostle Paul was referring to when he said, "For what can be known about God is plain to them [mankind], because God has shown it to them. For his invisible attributes, namely his eternal power and divine nature, have been clearly perceived, ever since the creation of the world, in things that have been made. So they are without excuse" (Rom 1:19-20). General revelation is what the Psalmist describes when he exclaims, "The heavens declare the glory of God, and the sky above proclaims his handiwork" (Ps 19:1). As joyous as this is, "the Light has come into the world [and] the people loved the darkness rather than the Light" (John 3:19). You see, God's general revelation is a problem to fallen man. Instead of praising God for this revelation to us, we try to figure out a way to reconcile nature with heaven and those unseen heavenly things that influence our very souls in a unified way that leaves God out.

It hasn't always been this way. Francis Schaeffer (1912–1984) was a Christian writer whose books and films dealt with the influence of culture on worldview and belief in God. He traced the origin of modern man to the end of the Byzantine era (1200s) and noted that up until that time, man's thought forms as reflected in art were not pictured realistically.[2] This was because heavenly things ("Grace," or "The Higher Things," in Schaeffer's terminology) were all-important and too holy to be depicted realistically. On the other hand, scenes of nature, such as trees, mountains and beaches ("Nature," or "The Lower Things"), held no interest for the artist. The first realistic landscape was painted in 1410 by Van Eyck. Schaeffer showed how from that point on the pendulum swung to the other extreme, with Nature completely pushing Grace out of the culture. Neither of these extremes is biblically sound. Neither is independent of the other. God is not in one dimension and man in the other. Jesus is equally Lord over Grace and Nature. The two dimensions are described in Figure 1.2.

2. Francis, *Escape from Reason*, 11–22.

Grace – The Higher

Nature – The Lower

Figure 1.2. "Grace," or "The Higher Things," including God the creator, heaven, and heavenly things, the unseen and its influence on the earth, man's soul, and unity vs. "Nature," or "The Lower Things," including the created, earth and earthly things, the visible, the activities of man and nature on earth, man's body, and diversity.

It's a similar idea to the box. Our sinful hearts go to great extremes to create an explanation that satisfies these two things while keeping us in control—or thinking we are. With the pretext of being rational, we irrationally limit explanations that reconcile heaven and earth in a unified way only to things of "Nature." We simply define things belonging to "The Higher" as being invalid explanations. By carefully crafting which assumptions to consider "valid" or "not valid," we convince ourselves that we can reconcile heaven and earth without God's help. For example, is an answer that could be explained by a miracle "valid"? Who determines "validity"? Of course, not everyone has pursued this line of thinking. The Reformers[3] recognized that general revelation points to special revelation, which is revelation embodied in the Bible as the Word of God,[4] and special revelation provides sufficient and final knowledge of the authority upon which general revelation (and all knowledge) rests. Special revelation completes and unifies. Special

---

3. The Reformers, or, "Protestant Reformers," were those who brought about a reformation of religion as practiced by the Roman Catholic Church in the years leading up to the 16th century. The Roman Catholic Church had fallen into corruption in many of their practices. They recognized the authority of Scripture alone, i.e.,—without the Pope or Roman Catholic Church as intermediaries between man and God.

4 Berkhof, *Systematic Theology*, 34-39.

revelation is through Christ alone, and "Christ" is not an empty word but a real, true Christ as revealed in Scripture. This is an important point because in today's world, words and names are used that often have been emptied of their true content and refilled with foreign content. For example, on a recent business trip I sat next to a colleague who adamantly told me he believed in Jesus but he didn't believe in the Bible. He had emptied the word "Jesus" of its content and blinded his eyes to God's revelation.

Special Revelation

As bleak as this denial of God's special revelation seems, our God is a long-suffering and merciful God. He created us as the mathematician Blaise Pascal said, with "a God-shaped vacuum in the heart . . . which cannot be filled by any created thing, but only by God, the Creator made known through Jesus."[5] So in spite of our willful turning from his Light, he does not leave us dead in our closed-minded sins of denial of his life and truth. No, he remembers and loves his children and gives us not only general revelation but also special revelation. He gave it in a person, Jesus Christ who came into the world in the flesh that his children could touch, speak, laugh and cry with, mourn for, and in time, glory with. God put on flesh to reveal himself in a special way to his children. "For God so loved the world, that he gave his only Son, that whoever believes in him should not perish but have eternal life. For God did not send his Son into the world to condemn the world, but in order that the world might be saved through him. Whoever believes in him is not condemned, but whoever does not believe is condemned already, because he has not believed in the name of the only Son of God" (John 3:16–18).

We aren't all there is. The natural world is not all there is. What our minds can contemplate is not comprehensive of infinity, of eternity; no, it is not even comprehensive of today's world or our own relationships and realities. What arrogance to think

---

5. Pascal, AZQuotes.com, quote 589335.

it is! Have you ever argued with someone about a topic that you were absolutely certain you were right about, only to have them show you something that hadn't occurred to you at all, and which completely changed your conclusion? Since we have all experienced this humbling in small things, why such arrogance in truly monumental things? But this isn't cause for despair. There is a reality, a truth which we yearn to connect with beyond our petty understanding. God is reaching his hand down to us right into the little box of our lives. He speaks to us if we but listen. "Today, if you hear his voice, do not harden your hearts as in the rebellion, on the day of testing in the wilderness" (Heb 3:7). This is what God is telling us: "Hear my voice! Do not harden your hearts to it!" And yet we do. Pride, arrogance, and unwillingness to submit to anything but our own desires all cause our hearts to harden. Our slavish obedience to these things is disobedience to God, and it stands between us and faith. Those without faith in the cleansing blood of Christ are left dead in their sins. They are condemned already. In the willful pursuit of the darkness of their sins they call true closed-mindedness "critical thinking" and true openness in minds and hearts to God they call closed-minded. Or, in the case of the current generation who is closed-minded and uninterested even in rationality and truth, the result is the same: "These people blaspheme all that they do not understand, and they are destroyed by all that they, like unreasoning animals, understand instinctively. Woe to them!" Jude says, "For they walked in the way of Cain and abandoned themselves for the sake of gain . . . These are hidden reefs, waterless clouds, swept along by winds; fruitless trees in late autumn . . . wild waves of the sea, casting up the foam of their own shame; wandering stars, for whom the gloom of utter darkness has been reserved forever" (Jude 10–13). Woe to us when we fall back to doubting God's reality. And we do doubt at times, don't we? We actually have an easier time believing his reality when contemplating those great mysteries of the universe than we do his reality in our daily lives. But we rarely contemplate those great mysteries of life anyway.

So we keep God tucked safely away in Schaeffer's compartment of Higher Things. But what about the everyday things that we think we control? Do you think about God's reality when you are fixing breakfast? Is he there when you're rushing to get the kids off to school and you've burnt the toast? Is his reality something you contemplate when you are out fishing? The Puritans expected to find him in all these little activities.[6] They would find him in the barn while they were milking the cow. The "Higher Things" and the everyday "Lower Things" are unified in the person of Christ. When we accept him as our Savior, we too are unified with the higher, eternal things and our everyday life activities are linked with the timeless. When we acknowledge this, even the small things take on the greater significance they should. And we work with the anticipation of hearing, "Well done good and faithful servant. You have been faithful over a little; I will set you over much. Enter into the joy of your master" (Matt 25:23).

Our Master is faithful to us in the little things, as well as the big. That may seem strange to us, but it shouldn't. After World War II the Japanese developed some techniques that improved their manufacturing efficiencies and quality so much that it transformed whole industries and caused them to leapfrog over even those countries who won the war. They would look for even small improvements of seconds.[7] Why? Because they knew that by improving a few seconds here and a few seconds there, they would soon save minutes and accumulating minutes would save hours and days. Attention to the little things transformed the automotive industry and others for at least a generation. God cares for his creation the same way. No sparrow falls without his knowledge (Luke 12:6). He takes a deep, personal interest in every detail of our lives. It's these "little" things, these "inconsequential" things that shape

---

6. "Puritan" was a derogatory name given to a group of people in sixteenth and seventeenth century England who sought further reformation in the Church of England. They began migrating to American in the early 1600s. They have been maligned as having, " . . . the haunting fear that someone, somewhere, may be happy." (Ryken, *Worldly Saints*, 1.) But this is grossly unfair. They looked for spiritual renewal in their lives and in society.

7. DeCarlo, *Lean Six Sigma*, 3–22.

us and make us who we are. These things that we might think God is too busy for reflect the state of our hearts. It is through these that the clay is shaped in the loving Master's hands for just the purpose he intended from before the foundation of the world (Eph 1:4–10; Isa 64:8). It's through these that he sanctifies us a little bit each day.

I recently flew to Europe. I got on the plane from Atlanta with a ticket for Amsterdam. That plane, like every other one that flies, was off course 90 percent of the time. How does it arrive at its destination? It veers a bit to the left, a bit to the right, but through it all, the pilot keeps bringing it back on course. He adjusts first this way, then that way. I didn't worry about my destination. I trusted the pilot to see me safely there, even though I was off course most of the time. Jesus is our pilot through life. With Christ as our destination, the Holy Spirit brings us back on course again and again; though we may drift 90 percent of the time. When we do contemplate God's reality in the things that we think are inconsequential, we begin to realize that the God of the universe is paying attention to even *me*! He sees me lose patience and chastens me. He knows my desires, but he also knows what I really want and need better than I do and gives me what I need to obtain them.

Steve Jobs, founder and long-time CEO of Apple, famously said the customer is *not* always right. He doesn't know what he wants until you show it to him.[8] What's true for an electronic gadget is so much more so for a life in eternity. God knows what we really want and is preparing that place for us in our eternal home. If we stop and consider our very personal God, is it any wonder we have more difficulty understanding his intimate, personal reality than his metaphysical reality that explains those monumental questions of life? When we consider it, we, like David, ask, "Who am I O Lord God . . . that you have brought me thus far?" (2 Sam 7:18). Yet he does pay attention to us in all that we do. We don't live enough of our waking hours with this realization, and it's to our loss and detriment. Our fears and anxieties result from forgetting this. When we look for him at all, we look for him in the "big" things. And, we fail to hear that "still small voice" right

---

8. Isaacson, *Steve Jobs*, 43.

beside us (1 Kgs 19:12). What is truly special in special revelation is how personal God is in his caring for us individually, how he has come to us and meets us in our everyday lives. The following chapters explore God's revelation and relationship to us as we learn to better recognize his hand upon us, leading and guiding us to glorify him and enjoy him forever,[9] until he calls us home.

Study Questions:

1. What is general revelation?
2. What is special revelation?
3. Can you give examples of the revelation of Christ in your daily life?
4. How does revelation bring together two worlds that seem contradictory—physical and spiritual?

---

9. Westminster Divines, *Westminster Confession of Faith*, 287.

2

How Do We Know What We Know?

"The fear of the Lord is the beginning of knowledge"

—PROV 1:7

Sequence of Turning Information Into "Knowledge"

LET ME TELL YOU about a mother turkey and a polecat. They are mortal enemies. Polecats kill turkey chicks, so mother turkeys hate them and will viciously attack them to protect her chirping little chicks. In fact, she will attack even if a dead polecat is just dragged past her—but if you put a small recorder in a stuffed polecat so it chirps like her baby chicks, *she gathers it under her wings and protects it!*[1] The chirping sound triggers an acceptance and protective response in the mother turkey even to her mortal enemy.

If you think this is merely an amusing story about a bird-brained animal, you're wrong. We have our own triggers that are constantly being pushed by marketers, politicians and generally anyone that wants to influence us—which is basically everyone. By understanding how our triggers work and what assumptions they are based on, we can better understand the validity of what

1. Cialdini, *Influence*, 2–3.

we think we know. And what we think we know is what we base our life's decisions on.

When we encounter something new, whether it's an idea, a way of doing something, or an experience, we want evidence to confirm what we think we understand about it. We file that evidence away in our mind as an assumption so that the next time we encounter that new thing, or something similar, we apply our assumption to it. If we go through this cycle repeatedly, it forms a habit, which is simply a conditioned response. We no longer need to think about what we do when we delegate our actions to habits; it's how we deal with an overwhelming barrage of information, or simply with information we don't find interesting enough to rethink the assumptions we have as its basis. This basic sequence of newness → evidence → assumption → habit and response is how we come to "know" things. The apostle Thomas had never known anyone to rise from the dead. Jesus had explained that he would, but it simply remained unbelievable to Thomas. He wanted to touch the nail scars in Jesus' hands and the wound in his side before he would believe (John 21:25). He wanted evidence that his mind could relate to his other experiences. Believing that someone could rise from the dead would upset not only the assumption he had about dead people staying dead, but it would also completely alter many of the assumptions he based his daily living on. It would fundamentally change his worldview and was just too much for him to deal with.

When I first got a touchscreen phone, everything was so new compared with the old phone. I had heard that I could tap the glass, move my finger around on it and do all kinds of things. I could write messages, take pictures, make phone calls, and more. When I got one in my hands I tried all these things. For me the first few times were so novel and amazing that I would repeat them just for fun. It was mesmerizing to see things happen as I moved my finger over the glass. During that period when it was all new to me, I was open to learning—*from it!* Today, I rarely give it a second thought. I expect it to work in a certain way and if the response isn't flawless, I get irritated. The novelty and wonder of it are gone.

How Do We Know What We Know?

I expect certain things to happen when I touch the screen because they are habits now. This way of knowing is well understood.

Politicians and marketers use it all the time. It's what branding is built upon. If they can first present us with something that will seem new enough to us to trigger the sequence of newness → evidence → assumption → habit and response, they can begin their work. Then they provide us with something—anything!—that we will accept as evidence. "Evidence" doesn't have to be truthful at all. We don't even have to believe its truthfulness. The key is that it is *accepted* by us. If we want to believe the messenger, or if we don't want to be bothered by complex or unpleasant subjects, we may accept something as "evidence" anyway. Then this so-called "evidence" is given repeatedly until we tire of challenging it in our minds and it becomes an assumption. With the assumption in place, our habit is formed and our response is assured. Think of a stopped drain – what comes to mind? "Call Roto-Rooter, that's the name, and away go troubles down the drain!" So we pick up the phone and we call Roto-Rooter.

Steven Covey, author of the tremendously popular book *The 7 Habits of Highly Effective People*[2] said there's a gap between stimulus and response. What we do in that brief gap is very important and depends almost entirely on the assumptions that we consciously or unconsciously apply to it. As Covey says, "The ability to subordinate an impulse to a value is the definition of a proactive person." We have plenty of impulses. Which ones have we put into our "impulse toolbox" through habits to apply at the moment when they are needed? What values went into establishing that "impulse toolbox"? How do those tools improve our "response-ability"? Hopefully, these tools are built from the study of the Bible, because they are proven and have stood the test of time. They are the very tools God himself has provided to us so we can glorify him and enjoy him forever,[3] and in so doing, find our own fulfillment

---

2. Covey, *7 Habits of Highly Effective People*, 70–72.

3. This is man's chief "end," or purpose, according to the Westminster Shorter Catechism, a teaching tool developed in the 1600s by church leaders and based on diligent study of the Bible. It is still being used today.

and happiness. It's our response that is essential. Our response determines our successes and failures in life. It determines how we experience life here and in eternity. Others want to control our response. The goal of marketing is not ultimately to get to us like a product; it's to get us to *buy* a product. The goal of kissing a baby or giving a speech is not to get us to like a politician so much as to get us to *vote* for him or her. Many people misunderstand the objective of propaganda. It isn't to get us to believe untruths. It is to get us to *respond* in a certain way.[4] Truths are always mixed with lies in the most effective propaganda. So how we think about "evidence" is critically important to us personally. It forms our assumptions. Our assumptions, conscious or unconscious, are the basis for our responses to life. And our responses to life form the basis for our success, contentment and happiness.

The sequence of newness → evidence → assumption → habit that leads us to a response or action is the way we are wired to interact with our world. So, let's spend a few minutes with each.

Newness

The sequence must begin with newness. Why is this? It gets our attention in a special way that familiarity doesn't. We can't resist bright, shiny things. We turn our attention to something new in a special way, without preconceptions; there is only one chance to make a first impression. That's why "new" and "different" are used together so often, yet are largely redundant. If I want someone to buy my improved paper towel, I must first defeat their assumption that it is just a paper towel. That assumption places it into a category that doesn't merit a different response: It's a paper towel. I buy my brand of paper towel. There is no need to change. Calling it "different" may generate a response—a yawn. It's still a paper towel. But calling it "new" is almost magical: It looks like any other paper towel—but is it? We give novelty the benefit of the doubt

---

4. Ellul, *Propaganda*, 25.

and almost always pay attention until we find out what is new. We begin to look. It is only then that we are open to evidence.

Evidence: Science, Faith, and Knowing

What about the next step, "evidence"? Evidence if often associated with science. We think of the pursuit of science as the purest way to separate ourselves from our emotions and biases and get at the "cold hard facts"—the evidence. I'm trained as a scientist and held this assumption for most of my life. But is this true? There are actually many ways to get *valid* evidence. Remember, those who are only interested in our response don't care about the validity of evidence, only the acceptability. *We* should care about the validity. Another way to ask this is, "Which evidence is authoritative?" We'll come back to this issue of authority in chapter 4. In most cases in life, science *isn't* the best way to recognize valid evidence.

My wife and I have been married over twenty-eight years. Not one of the things that really matter about what we know of each other is based on science or use of the scientific method. If I tried to set aside my emotions about her and just deal with the cold, hard facts, I could describe her—about six feet tall, we don't talk about weight or age, about 90 percent water, and consisting of a skeletal framework covered by skin. Useless! In twenty-eight years of marriage, I can't think of a single important application for these scientific facts. Now let's contrast this with a different kind of knowledge, Biblical knowledge: "As water reflects the face, so the heart of man reflects the man" (Prov 27:19); "An excellent wife who can find? She is far more precious than jewels. The heart of her husband trusts in her" (Prov 31:10-11). Through these I gain knowledge and appreciation for her heart. "[I]n the Lord woman is not independent of man nor man of woman" (1 Cor 11:11) In this is knowledge of our interdependence. "Faithful are the wounds of a friend: profuse are the kisses of an enemy" (Prov 27:6). In this there is knowledge of how to respond to her criticism. "It is better to live in a corner of the housetop than in a house shared with a quarrelsome wife" (Prov 25:24). Moving right along... "He who finds a wife finds a good thing and obtains favor from the Lord" (Prov 18:22). "Two men are better than one because they have good reward for their toil. For if they fall, one will lift up his fellow" (Eccl 4:9–10). These verses give knowledge of our strength together. "Husbands, love your wives, as Christ loved the church and gave himself up for her . . . husbands should love their wives as their own bodies. He who loves his wife loves himself . . . Let each one of you love his wife as himself, and let the wife see that she respects her husband" (Eph 5:25, 28, 33). These verses teach the importance of love and respect for each other. "Hell hath no fury like a woman scorned." Ok, so that one's not Biblical, but I thought I'd throw it in anyway. It's got to be inspired! Then in First Peter, "Likewise, husbands live with your wives in an understanding way, showing honor to the woman as the weaker vessel, since they are heirs with you of the grace of life, so that your prayers may not be hindered" (1 Pet 3:7). These and many more are ways of knowing that have real life application. They are based on many generations of accumulated evidence, the knowledge of our forebears, that we call tradition. They are based on how we are made. But more importantly, they obtain their validity, their authority, from God's Word. What greater evidence is needed?

As believers we understand this. But non-believers will say that this validity is no validity at all—it is faith-based, therefore it is based on emotion, superstition and the collective superstitions of our ancestors. They say, "We are more enlightened today. We have science to help us sort through those biases and find the truth." I want to let you in on a little secret. The advancement of science is faith-based too! The eminent scientist, Michael Polanyi, a friend of no less a scientist than Albert Einstein, came to this conclusion and wrote about it in several rather difficult to read books, such as *Personal Knowledge*.[5] What does he mean that the advancement of science is faith-based? I can only attempt to hit the high points here. Drusilla Scott provides a readable summary of Polanyi's work.[6] First of all, there is a reality that exists beyond

---

5. Polanyi, *Personal Knowledge*.

6. A much more readable summary is found in Drusilla Scott's, *Everyman*

How Do We Know What We Know?

our current state of knowledge and it is infinitely bigger and more comprehensive than our ability to conceive it. If we already knew all there is to know, there would be no need for science. Secondly, the reality is not randomness. There is design and pattern. If there weren't, probabilities, statistics and the scientific method that depends on them would be invalid and meaningless.

So a scientist pursuing a breakthrough must have faith in two things: 1. He can find a connection point that hasn't yet been made with this reality, and 2. The connection point is to be found where others aren't looking. If everyone knows where the answer lies, it really isn't a breakthrough once it's demonstrated. He has to pursue his faith in where reality can be found in the face of ridicule and arguments to the contrary by other scientists. He has to have a deep commitment to his faith during years of patiently working to establish this breakthrough, this connection to the greater reality. And often under-appreciated is the fact that this faith must be fueled with a deep passion to connect with and understand this greater reality. The best scientists are *not* detached pursuers of cold, hard facts. They have hypotheses, beliefs, *biases* that they follow with great energy and passion. None other than Charles Darwin said, "How odd it is that anyone should not see that all observation must be for or against some view if it is to be of any service!"[7] The scientist must care deeply! The idea that religious, Christian faith distorts our ability to think deeply and only scientists can put their feelings and biases aside and face reality without emotion so that facts and truth can be arrived at is nonsense. All scientists are human and have biases and emotions. Good scientists have the faith, passion and commitment to pursue their beliefs. They build upon the scientific evidence of their forebears—call it "scientific traditions." It is a conceit that the only valid evidence to connect with this greater reality is gained through scientific methods and this conceit not only artificially limits the scientist's data, but the very claim is self-defeating and impossible. Rationality itself is based on faith—faith that it is the means to connect with the un-

---

Revived: *The Common Sense of Michael Polanyi.*

7. Stark, *The Victory of Reason*, 13.

known, greater reality. Successful scientists have a healthy grasp of reality. I'm not saying that one has to be a Christian to be a good scientist. Certainly there are many examples to the contrary, but I think it helps because the beginning of knowledge is the fear of the Lord (Prov 1:7). Why is that so? Validity of evidence. Authority of evidence. As creator and ruler of all things, there is no greater authority than the Lord God. Ultimately, there can only be one of two choices in authority of truth—God or man.

Assumption

This leads us to the next step in the knowledge process: assumption. So what of the fundamental assumption of the Bible as the source of knowledge; for example, "The fear of the Lord is the beginning of knowledge" (Prov 1:7) and "I am the Way and the Truth and the Life" (John 14:6)? I think it is now quite clear that holding a worldview rooted in the Christian faith definitely does not preclude a person from knowing truth, as is often asserted in today's society. Not only is it asserted; it is forced upon us and our children. The smallest references to God have largely been purged in our schools, not only from science classes, but even from subjects like reading and writing, where the importance of Biblical knowledge used to be upheld routinely. Just look at a McGuffey's Reader[8] to see what I mean. Yet being a Christian is not only an asset in obtaining knowledge and knowing truth; it is the greatest possible asset. Faith in Jesus Christ is our connection to that greater reality, which is God. He is the Way and the Truth and the Life (John 14:6). Science actually emerged from this recognition as a pursuit for God's face in his creation. Many of the great scientists of history explicitly admitted this, as the very small sampling below shows.

Robert Boyle was a physicist, as well as the chemist credited with founding modern chemistry. He said, "God [is] the author of

---

8. McGuffey Readers were widely-used textbooks for grades 1–6 for a hundred years—from the mid-1800s, well into the 1900s. They are still used today in some private schools and in homeschooling.

the universe, and the free establisher of the laws of motion."[9] Joseph H. Taylor, Jr. received the Nobel Prize in physics in 1993 for the discovery of the first known binary pulsar and for his work which supported the Big Bang theory. He said, "A scientific discovery is also a religious discovery. There is no conflict between science and religion. Our knowledge of God is made larger with every discovery we make about the world."[10] Sir Isaac Newton, whom many regard as the greatest scientist the world has ever produced, said, "I have a fundamental belief in the Bible as the Word of God, written by those who were inspired. I study the Bible daily."[11] Albert Einstein said, "The more I study science, the more I believe in God."[12] Gregor Mendel, father of modern genetics, was an Austrian monk.[13] Einstein may have best captured how science emerged from faith in God: "I want to know how God created this world. I am not interested in this or that phenomenon, in the spectrum of this or that element. I want to know his thoughts; the rest are details."[14] Contrast this with the view of Joseph Goebbels, Nazi Minister of Propaganda and close associate of Adolf Hitler: "A church that does not keep step with modern scientific knowledge is doomed."[15]

Arguments of the incompatibility of Christianity and science are nothing more than modern examples of the age-old cosmic battle between the seed of the woman and the seed of the serpent (Gen 3:15). This foundational verse for Christianity is an immediate consequence of what is known as the Fall of Man. God had placed Adam and Eve in paradise and given them everything needed to be happy, including a personal relationship with him. The one commandment he gave them was to refrain from eating of the fruit of the Tree of the Knowledge of Good and Evil. If they did, they would

9. Boyle, AZQuotes.com, quote 587232.
10. Taylor, AZQuotes.com, quote 587231.
11. Newton, AZQuotes.com, quote 575505.
12. Holt, "Science Resurrects God," *The Wall Street Journal*, December 24, 1997.
13. Mendel, *Experiments in Plant Hybridisation*. v.
14. Jammer, *Einstein and Religion*, 123.
15. Metaxas, *Bonhoeffer*, 166.

surely die (Gen 2:16–17). But Satan, in the form of a serpent, convinced Adam and Eve to disobey God, causing them to fall away from him and bringing death into the world. Satan did this by placing doubt of God's words in the minds of Adam and Eve, asking Eve, "Did God actually say, 'You shall not eat of any tree in the garden?'" (Gen 3:1). Then he directly contradicted God's command and tempted them with God-like power, saying that if they ate the forbidden fruit, "You will not surely die. For God knows that when you eat of it your eyes will be opened, and you will be like God, knowing good and evil" (Gen 3:4–5). As a consequence of the Fall, God put enmity between the spiritual offspring ("seed," or followers) of the serpent, and the offspring of the woman. Though fallen, the seed of the woman would be redeemed to their former status as God's children over time through his mercy and grace.

Claims that Christianity and science are incompatible are merely attempts to undermine God's authority, the validity of the evidence he provides to all: "For the wrath of God is revealed from heaven against all ungodliness and unrighteousness of men, who by their unrighteousness suppress the truth. For what can be known about God is plain to them, because God has shown it to them. For his invisible attributes, namely, his eternal power and divine nature, have been clearly perceived, ever since the creation of the world, in the things that have been made. So they are without excuse" (Rom 1:18–20). The assertion and assumption that science is the only valid way to understand creation is Satan's attempt to convince us, as he did Eve, "God didn't really say," that man does not need to listen to God's words.

Response

We've talked about three of the four steps involved in how we know: the need for newness to get our attention with an open mind, the need for valid evidence, and the ability of valid evidence to solidify our assumptions. But knowledge that doesn't elicit a response is dead. Knowledge is a building block to action that makes us effective and fruitful: "For as the body apart from the spirit is dead, so also faith apart from works is dead" (Jas 2:26). We've discussed how we "know" what we think we know, so what is our response? Are we living reactively without knowledge, as a bug responds to light? Or are we conscious about our assumptions and the authority behind them? Are we frequently coming to new recognitions of our need for a Savior and finding new ways of dying to self and the belief that we, apart from God, can know anything about the things that really matter? Jesus gets our attention and leads us to himself. And he has surrounded us with evidence of himself: "The heavens declare the glory of God and the sky above proclaims his handiwork. Day to day pours out speech, and night to night reveals knowledge" (Ps 19:1–2). And if that weren't enough, he put on flesh, came into the world and lived among us. He left us with the evidence of his life, death and resurrection in scripture. As he breathed the universe into being, he also breathed his Word into scripture for teaching and equipping us for every good work (2 Tim 3:16). This is what fills the gap between stimulus and response in the Christian heart. So when we respond, we respond with "the assurance of things hoped for, the conviction of things not seen" (Heb 11:1). Our response is knowledge-based, evidence-based faith in the person of Jesus Christ, the Son of God: "By faith we understand that the universe was created by the Word of God, so that what is seen was not made out of things that are visible" (Heb 11:3). Our knowledge is based on the evidence and authority of God, so when he calls, we answer, "Here I am" (Isa 6:8). And our responses—whether in this life or the next—are fruitful. So how do we know what we know? By the fear of God and faith in Christ, The Truth, the Way and the Life, the One who lights our path and gives us knowledge.

Study Questions:

1. Explain the sequence of turning information into "knowing." newness → evidence → assumption → habit and response

2. How do science and faith relate to knowing?

3. What should be our response to knowing?

3

Obedience

"The road to faith passes through obedience to the call of Jesus."

—DIETRICH BONHOEFFER[1]

"Take care lest you forget the Lord your God by not keeping his commandments and his rules and his statutes . . . lest when you have eaten and are full and have built houses and live in them, and when your herds and flocks multiply and your silver and gold is multiplied and all that you have is multiplied, then your heart be lifted up, and you forget the Lord your God . . . Beware lest you say in your heart, 'My power and the might of my hand have gotten me this wealth.' You shall remember the Lord your God, for it is he who gives you power to get wealth, that he may confirm his covenant that he swore to your fathers . . . And if you forget the Lord your God and go after other gods and serve them and worship them, I solemnly warn you today that you shall surely perish. Like the nations that the Lord makes to perish before you, so you shall perish, because you would not obey the voice of the Lord your God" (Deut 8:11–20).

---

1. Bonhoeffer, *The Cost of Discipleship*.

Turning From Obedience

AMERICA WAS FOUNDED AS a Christian nation. The Pilgrims and Puritans came to America seeking a place of freedom to worship. Our Declaration of Independence states that man was endowed by his creator with certain unalienable rights. And when our government was formed, its founding document, the Constitution, was acknowledged as being suitable "only for a moral and religious people" and was "wholly inadequate to the government of any other."[2] Throughout history our Christian faith has been a common bond in American society, but this has eroded in recent years. There is a depressing litany of recent changes in American society that illustrate the erosion of our Christian founding. To illustrate a few we only need to ask how we came to the point in which high school valedictorians can lose their degree by mentioning God in their graduation speech, the Ten Commandments are removed from public places, and children are expelled from school for bringing their Bibles. How did this happen? It happened as it has happened so many times over the history of mankind. We forgot our God, as the Israelites were warned in Deuteronomy. We took a familiar route to get here. As the demon in C.S. Lewis's *The Screwtape Letters* says, "[W]e trod the safest road to Hell, the gradual one, with gentle slope, soft underfoot, without sudden turnings, without milestones, without guideposts."[3] While God was blessing us with peace and prosperity, we were not obedient to him. Our faith was a shallow faith which is always accompanied by a superficial obedience. Just a couple of generations ago, Germany was at a similar place.

The German church was under siege from within and from without. Seeds of evil had sprouted and were growing rapidly. Christianity as it was practiced was superficial and rotten. An earnest young German pastor, Dietrich Bonhoeffer, was troubled

---

2. John Adams, Message from John Adams to the officers of the First Brigade of the Third Division of the Militia of Massachusetts, October 11, 1798. Adams. AZQuotes.com, quote 1936.

3. Lewis, *Screwtape Letters*, 61.

by what he saw. He felt that what was especially missing from the life of Christians in Germany was the day-to-day reality of dying to self. This Christian concept describes both a one-time turning over our lives to Christ and being "born again," as well as a lifetime progression of turning more and more from the things of this world and towards Christ, of following Christ with every ounce of one's being in every moment, in every part of one's life. Aren't there parallels to Bonhoeffer's Germany today? How can we grow in our dying to self while becoming increasingly strident in asserting "victim" status over more and more petty slights? How can we grow in our dying to self while celebrating empty vanities in others? For example, it is quite common today to be lionized and famous, not for anything you've accomplished, but simply because you are famous—think Kardashians.

In much of Christianity, we are content in our comforts as God warned against in Deuteronomy—safe in our borrowed freedom, smug in our own righteousness. Our worldly comforts can be obstacles to receiving God's grace: "It is easier for a camel to go through the eye of a needle than for a rich person to enter the kingdom of God" (Matt 19:24). Young Bonhoeffer described this as "cheap grace," grace that requires merely mental assent. The churches in Germany were not preaching the need for repentance from sin. Yet, in the face of sin, in the face of evil, "the Gospel is protected by the preaching of repentance which calls sin sin and declares the sinner guilty."[4] Repentance requires a change of heart, but if sincere, the change of heart will be expressed in changed actions. In societies where Christians are not persecuted, changed actions come at little cost and all too often are like the seed scattered on stony ground—they are poorly rooted and quickly wither (Matt 13:3–9).

Bonhoeffer lived in Germany during a time when personal stakes were very high. He was involved in a conspiracy to kill Hitler for which he was imprisoned and later executed. What would you do in his shoes? The Bible teaches that lying is wrong, killing is wrong. Yet God asks us to live and act in obedience to him in a fallen world (John 17:15). Bonhoeffer wrestled greatly with this. From

---

4. Metaxas, *Bonhoeffer*, 293.

prison he wrote the essay *What Does It Mean to Tell the Truth?* In it he argued that God's standard of truth entailed more than merely not lying. Jesus took the Old Testament laws to a deeper level of meaning and obedience from the "letter of the Law" to the "spirit of the Law."[5] In the Sermon on the Mount (Matthew 5–7), Jesus used a series of contrasts with the refrain, "You have heard that it was said . . . But I say to you." For example, he said, "You have heard that it was said to those of old, 'You shall not murder; and whoever murders will be liable to judgment.' But I say to you that everyone who is angry with his brother will be liable to judgment" (Matt 5:21–22). If we breathe a sigh of relief that we are not presently living, as Bonhoeffer did, as a Christian in World War II Germany, in which obedience to God may require unavoidable life-or-death decisions, we deceive ourselves. In one sense war brings to our conscience the inescapability of our decisions of obedience to God or not. This *is* the reality of life! We do not escape our decisions to obey God or not. Ours is the more perilous situation in which we aren't forced to recognize our utter dependence on Christ moment-by-moment, day-by-day as in wartime. Our fate creeps up on us slowly, quietly until we too late recognize our anguish and like the rich man in the story of Lazarus, are desperate for relief (Luke 16:19–31). In attempting to escape the reality of our need to be obedient, we are just those travelers that the demon Screwtape speaks of. We tread the safest road to Hell.

Bonhoeffer, in describing different ways people try to deal with evil, says, "[T]here are some who retreat to a 'private virtuousness.' Such people neither steal, nor murder, nor commit adultery. But . . . they must close their eyes and ears to the injustice around them. Only at the cost of self-deception can they keep their private blamelessness clean from the stains of responsible action in the world. In all that they do, what they fail to do will not let them rest."[6] This realization no doubt has spawned the "social justice" movement in liberal churches. Think of James (the earthly brother of Jesus and the leader of the Jerusalem church) stating, "Faith

5. Ibid., 365-366.
6. Ibid., 470.

without works is dead" (Jas 2:26)—not because of the value of the works, but because of the obedience to God's will. And this is what the social justice churches forget. They talk a lot about Jesus' teaching and not so much about the reality of his Resurrection, or obedience to God through faith in Christ. Obedience is not to a social cause, but to God through the person of the Son of God, Jesus Christ. When Mary poured expensive nard on Jesus and was scolded by the apostles, Jesus said, "[Y]ou always have the poor with you" (Matt 26:11). He was acknowledging that in this fallen world, there will always be poor people. Obedience to solving poverty, for example, is not *primary*. Of course it is important and our duty; Jesus over and over admonishes us to give to the poor. But obedience to God is what is *primary*.

Turning To Obedience

Bonhoeffer explains this, saying, "The road to faith passes through obedience to the call of Jesus. Unless a definite step is demanded, the call vanishes into thin air, and if men imagine that they can follow Jesus without taking this step, they are deluding themselves."[7] Levi left his tax collector's desk, Peter left his fishing nets—they took definite steps following Jesus' call. Did their step save them? No! But it created for them a new situation. They were no longer sitting at their desk or working at their nets, observing Jesus as a phenomenon, someone who they saw doing good deeds and causing them to think religious thoughts. When they stepped away from their world in obedience to his call, they were placed in a new relationship with him, one in which it became possible to see him as God incarnate. Prior to obedience he was someone to observe, contemplate and evaluate as an object external to us. After initial obedience, staking everything on him becomes a matter of degree. In theological language we would say that prior to obedience we were unrepentant, dead in our sins. At obedience, we are regenerated by the work of the Holy Spirit and repent and accept

---

7. Bonhoeffer, *Cost of Discipleship*, 62–63.

Jesus as our Lord and Savior with a saving faith. Post-obedience we recognize the futility of our personal accomplishments and works and rest in the finished work of Christ. Before obedience, we sit at our desks and work at our nets with a self-centered detachment from the rest of the world that says, "It is I who live . . . it is I who will determine what is moral and just and fair . . . It is I who will determine how I will live and treat others." In short, it is an outlook in which everyone does what is right in his own eyes (Judg 17:6). Obedience is to act in accord with another's wishes, not our own. By taking that first step in obedience we move from the world of "It is I who live . . . it is I who will determine" to the world of "it is he who lives . . . it is he who will determine." So this is the new situation that is created by obedience. It opens the possibility to the heretofore foreign situation in which we stake everything in our lives on Jesus' Word. Post-obedience we say with Paul, "It is no longer I who live, but Christ who lives in me. And the life I now live in the flesh I live by faith in the Son of God" (Gal 2:20).

Following Christ

Once Peter took that first step of obedience and left his fish nets to follow Jesus, he was proclaiming through his action to all who knew him—his father, his brothers, his friends and neighbors, his family—that his life was being reordered. No longer would his first obedience be to those things that he and they were accustomed to being put first. He would follow Jesus! This is a bold statement. It's life-changing by definition and hard to believe for those who knew what our priorities were before. But of course the new life of obedience has only just begun. We often find ourselves like Paul: "For I do not understand my own actions. For I do not do what I want, but I do the very thing I hate" (Rom 7:15–25).

Bonhoeffer says, "It is only the call of Jesus which makes our obedience a situation where faith is possible."[8] Without a call, there is nothing to be obedient to. Once we are called, our faith is

---

8. Ibid., 63.

expressed in obedience. "[A] situation where faith is possible can never be demonstrated from the human side. Discipleship is not an offer man makes to Christ. It is only the call which creates the situation." Though we are all fallen and sinful, by God's grace and mercy, he creates the situation where a saving faith is possible. "[T]he situation in which faith is possible is itself only rendered possible through faith . . . only he who believes is obedient, and only he who is obedient believes." Marriage is one example of a gift God has given us that gives some insight into what Bonhoeffer is saying, though it is between two fallen people. By committing yourself to your spouse for life through marriage, a situation is created for faith to be expressed and deepen over time. Here faith, as expressed in trust—at times undeserved trust—and obedience not to a person, but to marriage vows (and therefore, to God), over time brings out the best in each. With the easy divorces and non-committal relationships of today, faith and obedience in marriage aren't given opportunity to do their work. This isn't a perfect analogy, but it's one that many of us have experience with. To avoid the difficulties in thinking about this in terms of faith and obedience between two fallen people, think about it in the way Jesus spoke to Peter.

> "When they had eaten breakfast, Jesus said to Simon Peter, 'Simon, son of John, do you love me more than these?' He said to him, 'Yes, Lord; you know that I love you.' He said to him, 'Feed my lambs.' He said to him a second time, 'Simon, son of John, do you love me?' He said to him, 'Yes, Lord; you know that I love you.' He said to him, 'Tend my sheep.' He said to him the third time, 'Simon, son of John, do you love me?' Peter was grieved because he said to him the third time, 'Do you love me?' and he said to him, 'Lord, you know everything; you know that I love you.' Jesus said to him, 'Feed my sheep. Truly, truly I say to you, when you were young, you used to dress yourself and walk wherever you wanted, but when you are old, you will stretch out your hands, and another will dress you and carry you where you do not want to go.' (This he said to show by what kind of death he was to glorify God.) And after saying this he said to him, 'Follow me.' Peter turned and saw the disciple whom Jesus

loved [John] following them . . . When Peter saw him, he said to Jesus, 'Lord, what about this man?' Jesus said to him, 'If it is my will that he remain until I come, what is that to you? You follow me!'" (John 21:15–22)

Jesus posed the same question three times to Peter. He asked the first time, "Do you love me more than these?" Peter answered as we often do our spouse, without giving it much thought, taking the magnitude of the answer lightly: "Yes, Lord; you know that I love you." That is followed, as is often the case in marriage and other relationships, with a request to act on what we've said. Feed my lambs. How often do we even give this a second thought? If we're busy, we may be a bit irritated by it but we do what's asked anyway to show that we do indeed love her (or him). It's not that big a deal. Obedience is at little cost.

But then Jesus asked a second time and more formally, "Simon, son of John, do you love me?" Did your parents ever use your full name to let you know the seriousness of the situation just got greater? "Brett Callaway don't you ever do that again!" Jesus is getting Peter's attention, letting Peter know he was being called to a situation for which an easy, thoughtless obedience will not be sufficient. Peter now has to pause and give some considered thought. But thought to what? This is a very difficult answer, not because the answer is unclear, but because the answer is so obvious and so contrary to the answer we want. It is an answer which we desperately want to ignore. The answer is obedience. Feed my lambs. Obey. Only he who is obedient believes, only he who believes is obedient. This is what Jesus is saying: "Do you love me? Do you believe I am who I am?" (The long-awaited Messiah—the Christ).[9] Then obey!

Bonhoeffer points to the case of the rich young man in Matthew 19:16–22 who comes to Jesus and asks, "Teacher, what good deed must I do to have eternal life?"[10] He approaches God incarnate as merely a teacher. He's looking for an intellectual answer. He's attempting to engage with Jesus in an academic conversation resulting

---

9. Peter had earlier (Matt 16:16) confessed that Jesus was the Christ.
10. Bonhoeffer, *Cost of Discipleship*, 70–76.

in a philosophical answer. How does Jesus respond? "Why do you ask me about what is good? There is only one who is good." He confronts the man with who Jesus is. It is essentially a question of faith: "Do you recognize and acknowledge who I am?" Then after reciting the intellectual answers that the man clearly already knew, Jesus gives the answer that the man didn't want to hear, "Follow me," obey, walk away from the world in which you live in the false security of your possessions—just obey, sell them, follow me.

Isn't this the case in our lives? It may be that this is even more pertinent to us when we are very diligent about the intellectual side of our faith but less so about applying it. We may be quite knowledgeable about correct doctrine. But do we hide behind it to avoid obeying? Look at how faith and obedience were one in Abraham. When God gave him the commandment to circumcise his household, he did it the very next day (Gen 17:23). When God told Abraham to sacrifice his son Isaac, he went the very next morning (Gen 22:1–14). Bonhoeffer gives the example of a church member speaking to his pastor, who is concerned that he's falling away from his faith.[11] The pastor says, "You should come to church, listen to the Word." The man says, "I do, but it just doesn't have much effect. It falls on deaf ears." The pastor says, "It's because you don't really want to listen." The man responds, "No, really I do." And this is where the conversation usually ends. Obedience is forgotten. Obedience doesn't stop, or in some cases even start, with going to church. If a sermon or Sunday school lesson is an intellectual exercise in which God's Word is only something to be speculated upon, evaluated by our criteria and subjected to our doubts and reservations, obedience can be postponed or avoided. As long as we can create questions that we require answers to before acting, we avoid obedience to God. We stay in control. We say, "We will be obedient to you, Lord, just as soon as you satisfy my question about this." But then, of course we have another question for him. Bonhoeffer says, "The devil has an answer to our moral difficulties:

---

11. Ibid., 69.

'Keep on posing problems, and you will escape the necessity of obedience.'"[12]

Jesus can ask us once, "Do you love me?" We have our easy answer. We do. We show it by going to church, reading his Word, and proclaiming his name. Then he asks again, "Do you love me?" What does he *want*? We've been obedient in all these things. But we know "He who asks for little receives little," so we step out further in obedience, where we feel like we're losing control. In fact, we never were in control. We learn deeper faith in our obedience. Then he asks again, "Do you love me?" How does he ask it? Perhaps, it's that dreaded phone call in the middle of the night of a terrible car wreck where we respond, "Oh, Lord no! Not this!" Perhaps he asks when the doctor comes into the room with a very solemn face and says, "I'm sorry, but your diagnosis is not good." Or, as it was with Bonhoeffer, the SS show up at the door and walk you to their car. We, like Peter, say, "Lord, you know everything; you know that I love you." And we also say, "Not this!" Jesus does know us, and he will never give us a burden we cannot bear, because he will bear it with us. He is our living reminder that the life and riches and peace of the resurrection was only found along the path of the cross. In the moment it is almost impossible to see, but it is there. He says to us in those moments, "Truly, truly, I say to you, when you were young, you used to dress yourself and walk wherever you wanted, but when you are old, you will stretch out your hands, and another will dress you and carry you where you do not want to go" (John 21:18). He then repeats, as he did to Peter, "Follow me."

In facing the madness everywhere around him and seeing his friends persecuted and killed, knowing that he too would soon be arrested and killed, Bonhoeffer said this: "In the whole of world history there is always only one really significant hour—the present . . . nowadays we often ask ourselves whether we still need the Church, whether we still need God. But this question is wrong. We are the ones who are questioned. The Church exists and God exists, and we are asked whether we are willing to be of service."[13]

---

12. Ibid., 73.
13. Metaxas, *Bonhoeffer*, 125.

Jesus did not only communicate ideas and concepts and rules and principles for living; he *lived*![14] He experienced the agony of the cross and he knows the glory of what lies beyond! We must take his outstretched hand in faith and obedience when our time comes to "feed his sheep." The times in the lives of men that are the most dreaded are also the greatest opportunities to show others the power of faith and obedience to see us through. They present some of the greatest opportunities to feed his sheep. Does that mean each one of us will be asked to walk the same path in this valley? No, it doesn't. Jesus has a purpose for each one of us, just as he did for Peter and John. When the Lord asked Peter to follow where he did not want to go, Peter looked at John and asked, "Lord, what about this man?" And Jesus said, "If it is my will that he remain until I come, what is that to you? You follow me!"

He who believes is obedient. He who is obedient believes. When Jesus says, "Feed my sheep" and "obey," what will you do? Peace in this life and eternal joy in the next are found by the saving blood of Christ and no other. As Bonhoeffer said, "The road to faith passes through obedience to the call of Christ." Though it lead through the valley of the shadow of death, I will fear no evil" (Ps 23:4). His rod and his staff comfort us. As the old hymn says, "For we never can prove the delights of his love until all on the altar we lay. For the favor he shows and the joy he bestows are for them who will trust and *obey*."[15]

When Dietrich Bonhoeffer was called from his Nazi prison cell to be led off for execution, he told his cell mate, "This is the end . . . for me the beginning of life."[16]

---

14. Ibid., 129.

15. Trust and Obey is found in Fettke, *Hymnal for Worship and Celebration*, 349.

16. Metaxas, *Bonhoeffer,* 528.

Study Questions:

1. Why do you think Bonhoeffer said, "The road to faith passes through obedience to the call of Jesus"?
2. What can we learn about our own lives from how the rich young man interacted with Jesus?

Westminster Shorter Catechism # 39[17]

Q: What is the duty which God requireth of man?

A: The duty which God requireth of man, is obedience to his revealed will.

---

17. Westminster Divines, *Westminster Confession of Faith*, 298.

4

Authority

"Jesus came and said to them, 'All authority in heaven and on earth has been given to me'"

—MATT 28:18

Our Problems With Authority

A SUBSTITUTE TEACHER IN Baltimore stopped a student in the hall who didn't have a hall pass. The student beat him unconscious, breaking the teacher's jaw.[1] This was just one of 873 student assaults[2] on teachers in just one school district in one year alone.[3] There is a serious lack of respect for teacher authority in today's schools. Miosotis Familia, a woman police officer was murdered while sitting in her patrol car—merely because she was a police

---

1. This was posted February 26, 2013 and updated February 28, 2013. Kuebler, "Student on teacher assaults on rise."

2. This number is lower than the actual assaults because it is the number that resulted in suspensions.

3. This article appeared in the online version of the Baltimore Sun, and was posted February 16, 2014. Green, Calvert and Broadwater, "Painful Lessons."

officer.[4] It is all too common for police officers to be targeted simply because they are police.[5] We have a very serious problem with respect for the authority of our law enforcement.

In recent years there have been millions of people pouring across our border illegally, many with the help of our own citizens. It has become commonplace for even the highest "public servants," as we used to know them, who take their oaths of office to uphold the laws of our land with hand upon the Bible, to pick and choose which laws they will enforce and which ones they will ignore. And there have been virtually no consequences for doing so. In fact, police are often told to "stand down" when lawlessness breaks out. We have a very serious problem with respect for the authority of our laws and the rule of law in general.

I could go on but you get the picture. The generation that lived out the slogan "question authority" has spawned an entire culture that has no concept of the necessity of respect for authority as the guardrail which stands between a civil, functioning society and anarchy. We are entering a dangerous place in which "everyone does what is right in their own minds" (Judg 21:25). "Authority" is often viewed as oppressive rather than a healthy stabilizer, though certainly the oppressive form also exists. What is the answer? Should authority be submitted to for the sake of a stable society, or resisted to throw off oppression? Where has mankind come closer to getting the answer right when we look back across human history? What have been the conditions under which humanity has enjoyed significantly less oppression by authority while maintaining a healthy degree of stability in society? Getting this right has been the overwhelming exception for mankind.

---

4. This article appeared in the online version of The New York Times, and was posted July 5, 2017. Mueller and Baker, "Police officer is 'murdered for her uniform."

5. Search engine algorithms seem to bury killings of police officers while highlighting instances of police shooting civilians. The real news is how police officers are now being targeted, merely for being police officers. Hayden, "4 officers shot within 24 hours amid violent year for police."

Historical Examples of Authority in Society

"American exceptionalism" is a term used to describe the fact that for much or our history, America was recognized the world over as having gotten the balance much better than most, perhaps any, other nation. France, at about the same time as America's birth, also made a monumental attempt to address the question of authority and how it is exercised, with disastrous results. Both nations made declarations of the basis and goals of their experiments.

Notice certain things about the French Declaration of the Rights of Man and the Citizen, as compared to the American Declaration of Independence.

The French document explains the revolution this way: "The representatives of the French people, organized as a national assembly, considering that *ignorance, neglect, and scorn of the rights of man are the sole causes of public misfortunes and of corruption of governments* [italics mine]."[6] The French Revolution was a child of The Enlightenment—a misnomer if there ever was one—where once again mankind attempted to create a utopia on earth and fulfill the words of the serpent in the Garden of Eden: "Ye shall be as gods" (Gen 3:5). Notice there is no mention of sin as being the cause of public misfortune or corruption of governments. No, they lay the causes for these problems as being within the abilities of man alone to solve, with greater knowledge and less ignorance, with greater attentiveness to the issues and to the rights of man, these misfortunes would vanish.

Contrast this to our own Declaration of Independence: "We hold these truths to be self-evident, that all men are created equal, that they are endowed by their Creator with certain unalienable rights, that among these are life, liberty and the pursuit of happiness. That to secure these rights governments are instituted among men." The writers close by stating their, "firm reliance on the protection of Divine Providence." While it couldn't be called a religious document, our Declaration is clearly infused with the realization of both our humble place before God and our glorious place as

---

6. Spielvogel, *Western Civilization*, 542.

his image-bearers. There are many such differences between the founding documents that gave birth to America versus those that gave birth to Revolutionary France. Both acknowledge men's freedom and their equality. But the French Declaration adds, "Social distinctions can be established only for the common benefit" (Article 1). There is no Biblical basis for this communistic sentiment. It is wholly absent from our Declaration. Another example is the French Declaration's statement, "Liberty consists in being able to do anything that does not harm another person" (Article 4). Contrast this with the statement by Thomas Jefferson, inscribed on the Jefferson Memorial: "The God who gave us life gave us liberty. Can the liberties of a nation be secure when we have removed a conviction that these liberties are the gift of God?" America had a very unique vision of her place in the world, a vision very different from that which today's history revisionists would have us believe. Another one of America's truly great presidents, Calvin Coolidge, said this at a speech honoring Bishop Francis Asbury—he made the basis for the success of America's government explicit—"Our government rests upon religion. It is from that source that we derive our reverence for truth and justice, for equality and liberty, and for the rights of mankind. Unless the people believe in these principles they cannot believe in our government. There are only two main theories of government in the world. One rests on righteousness, the other rests on force."[7]

The difference in who was acknowledged as the ultimate authority—God or man—was the fundamental difference in outcome of the two revolutions. In France, the Committee of Public Safety established the Reign of Terror[8]—Satan must have been gleeful at the irony! The Reign of Terror targeted internal enemies of the Revolution and butchered many thousands. When the guillotine didn't kill fast enough, citizens of all ages and sexes were put before cannons and blown into open graves by grapeshot. Contrary to popular opinion, the Reign of Terror was not limited to killing the nobility. They were only 8 percent of the victims. Peasants made up 60 percent and

7. Pietrusza, *Silent Cal's Almanac*, 100.
8. Spielvogel, *Western Civilization*, 546.

the middle class another 25 percent.⁹ The French Revolution also followed a de-Christianization policy.¹⁰ In practices reminiscent of what we have been seeing in recent years, words such as "saint" were removed from public places. Exactly as is being done today with the use of "BCE," years were no longer to be numbered from the birth of Christ. A new calendar was instituted that eliminated Sundays. Religious celebrations were to be replaced by Revolutionary festivals. As has been the norm in human history, France looked to the authority of man in building their new nation. But listen to John Adams, one of America's Founding Fathers and our second president, who stated in a letter to the Militia of Massachusetts, "We have no government armed with power capable of contending with human passions unbridled by morality and religion . . . Our Constitution was made only for a moral and religious people. It is wholly inadequate to the government of any other."[11]

Why would our founders have created a Constitution that they admit only works for a moral and religious people? Did they believe we were, or would be, particularly moral and religious? Not at all. But they did have the amazing clarity that this is mankind's only hope because they knew God's authority is man's only hope. They established our government upon the right foundation, unlike all others before. "For no one can lay a foundation other than that which is laid, which is Jesus Christ" (1 Cor 3:11). The alternative foundation based on man's authority sooner or later degenerates into despotism and tyranny. For most of our lives, the United States, Christianity and the remaining vestiges of Christian morals have stood in the breach between freedom and tyranny. Today, we are perilously close to rejecting God's authority in this country—then what?

Well, let's consider the recent history of what happens when governments reject God. The most comprehensive book on this topic that I am aware of is by R.J. Rummel, published in 1994.[12] He exhaustively documents murders from 1900 to 1988. These

9. Ibid., 547.
10. Ibid., 549–550.
11. Adams. AZQuotes.com, quote 1936.
12. Rummel, *Death By Government*.

aren't what we would call homicides. He calls them "democides."[13] He provides grisly, detailed documentation proving Lord Acton's contention, "Power tends to corrupt; absolute power corrupts absolutely."[14] Ranking democide by regime, democracies account for only 1 percent, authoritarian regimes account for 17 percent and totalitarian and communist regimes account for 82 percent of all murders.[15] Power, unrestrained by God's authority, inevitably leads to unrestrained evil. And who is this evil directed at? Are these killings the result of defending the homeland against foreign threats? Overwhelmingly, the answer is no! Of the conservative estimate of 203 million murders, "only" 17 percent (thirty-four million) are the result of war. An astonishing 83 percent (169 million) of the killings have been by government against their own citizens.[16] Rummel says it this way: "In total, during the first eighty-eight years of this century, almost 170 million men, women and children have been shot, beaten, tortured, knifed, burned, starved, frozen, crushed, worked to death; buried alive, drowned, hung, bombed, or killed in any other of the myriad ways governments have inflicted death on unarmed, helpless citizens. The dead could conceivably be nearly 360 million people, a number equal to the entire population of the United States."[17] And let's not forget that these numbers say nothing about lives lost by abortions – also sanctioned, funded, and in some countries required by government. Rummel says,

> "It is hard to imagine 1,000 killed, not to mention 1 million (Stalin conservatively killed 62 million of his own people). Perhaps a better way of comprehending this is in terms of the rough risk of a citizen's being killed by the Communist Party of China. Since 1949, conservatively

---

13. "The murder of any person or people by a government, including genocide, politicide, and mass murder." – Ibid., 31

14. Acton. AZQuotes.com. quote 1486. This famous quote was based on a letter to Bishop Mandell Creighton, 3 April 1887.

15. Rummel, *Death By Government*, 17.

16. For all the activism by the Left against war and gun ownership by the citizenry, where the vast majority of killing of innocents happens is via overpowerful government; something they actively agitate *for!*

17. Rummel, *Death By Government*, 9.

> almost one out of every twenty men, women, and children have been killed. Why all this ... democide? In each case, power was nearly absolute, the central tenets of Marxism [as] the bible, high communist officials its priests, the Communist Party its church, and the achievement of the Marxist heaven—communism—the ultimate goal. In each country, the same classes—bourgeoisie, priests, landlords, the rich, and officers and officials of the previous regime—were sinful, enemies of the Good. Capitalists and their offspring were especially evil."[18]

Think of how politicians and activists have similarly fragmented society into groups of "oppressors" and "victims" today. Rummel goes on to say,

> "The verdict for such class membership was often death. Moreover, belief in Marxism was so fanatical among communists in both systems, they were so sure that they knew the absolute truth, that they would brook no opposition, antagonism, or displeasure by intellectuals or the masses. Typical of Marxist parties, rigid, doctrinaire intolerance was considered a virtue."[19]

What of the rigid, doctrinaire intolerance we see today? It is being promoted and considered as a virtue and labeled "tolerance." Do you ever feel pressured to censor your own views on the environment, which bathroom to use, what produce to buy, which car to drive, which political party to support, how much salt to use, which statues to maintain, what words to speak or what thoughts to think? All around us a war is raging. Its battle lines have ebbed and flowed for a long, long time. And what is its fundamental basis? The same as in the Garden of Eden: "God didn't really say." The battle is based on the answer to the question of authority – God's authority, or man's.

---

18. Ibid., 101.
19. Ibid., 101.

AUTHORITY

Authority of God in Our Personal Lives

What's true for nations is also true for us as individuals. The question of authority is often posed as where to strike the balance between conformity to rules versus "freedom" and "self-expression." But these aren't choices that matter. If you conform to or deviate from man's authority for rules or self-expression, it's still based on man's authority. The anarchist is no more free than the government bureaucrat because they both use man's rules as their measure of freedom. We are either slaves to man or slaves to God, either slaves to sin or slaves to righteousness. It depends on the authority we submit to: "For when you were slaves of sin, you were free in regard to righteousness. But what fruit were you getting at that time from the things of which you are now ashamed? For the end of those things is death. But now that you have been set free from sin and have become slaves of God, the fruit you get leads to sanctification and its end, eternal life" (Rom 6:20–22).

We are still listening to the words, "God didn't really say." Words without proper authority behind them are perverse, deadly, even chillingly evil. "I love children" spoken by a kind grandmother is a beautiful expression. "I love children" spoken by a child molester is chillingly evil. "Greetings, Rabbi" were the words of Judas just before betraying Jesus to death with a kiss (Matt 26:49). The authority behind the words makes all the difference. We live in a world of lies, lies from those whose products we buy, lies from the officials we elect, fake news, fake images, manufactured rage, manufactured celebrity. We are drowning in propaganda and lies because we have lost sight of the truth: "[We have] exchanged the truth about God for a lie and worshipped and served the creature rather than the Creator" (Rom 1:25). "God is not man, that he should lie" (Num 23:19). "It is impossible for God to lie" (Heb 6:18). Jesus is the Way and the *Truth* and the Life (John 14:6). How can we follow him and continue to expose ourselves to the lies that pour out of our televisions and web pages? John warns us, "No lie is of the truth" (1 John 2:21). Jesus is the truth, the one true authority for our lives. Satan is the Father of Lies (John 8:44), the counterfeiter of all truth. He is the author and Bureau Chief of fake news. He is the counterfeit, the poseur of authority.

Why do we continue to turn on those founts of lies and turn away from the Fount of Every Blessing?[20] The remedy is repentance. Repent from turning from the Way and the Truth. Repent from following the counterfeit authority. Repent from the old habits and reflexive acceptance of lies. Repent, repent, repent all day every day; turn back again and again to Jesus. The choice is as old as humanity—"Did God really say?" or not? Do we believe in man and man alone, or Christ and Christ alone for our salvation? Do we hold to the lie of our own righteousness, or do we repent and include ourselves in the truth that "None is righteous, no, not one" (Rom 3:10). All authority in heaven and earth has been given to Jesus (Matt 28:18). Do you accept that? "Because if you confess with your mouth that *Jesus* is Lord and believe in your heart that God raised him from the dead, you will be saved" (Rom 10:9).

Just as I was at this point in writing this chapter I got a call from a neighbor, Steve, who had never before called just to talk. He's a little older than I am and has a grown daughter and a granddaughter. He told me that although he had been going to church for several years, neither his daughter nor son-in-law had been going to church. They weren't hostile to Christianity, but didn't think it was important enough to put ahead of all the other things in their lives. She hadn't given her life to God's authority. One afternoon Annie[21] picked up her daughter to go to a ballgame. As she was driving east on Interstate 40 she began to feel nauseous and lost consciousness. Her daughter managed to grab the steering wheel as they hit the guardrail. Once the car had stopped, she was able to call Steve and said they had been in a wreck and her momma wouldn't wake up. Steve and his wife raced to the scene, she still in her pajamas. He is trained as a first responder and he arrived just as the EMS arrived. He saw his daughter lying by the side of the road with her eyes open and set. He'd seen this many times before.

---

20. "Fount of Every Blessing" refers to Jesus Christ and is recalled in a popular hymn of this name. Fettke, *Hymnal*, 2.

21. Not her real name.

She was dead. About that time the air-lift arrived and they rushed her to the hospital in Asheville. Steve and his wife followed in their car feeling completely numb and hopeless. He was certain that they would be told to go home once they arrived. He kept quietly praying over and over in his big, gruff voice the whole way there, "Lord, please don't take my baby."

But God wasn't finished with Annie. The doctors had to drill a hole in her head to relieve pressure on her brain and saw some faint response in her vital signs. Steve was told that she would have at least three months of rehab and permanent brain damage. Three *weeks* later she walked out of the hospital with only some numbness in her little toe. Annie has no doubt whatsoever that this miracle was God's work. She has given him authority over her life. Today she is very active in her church. She teaches children's Sunday school and shares her story so others will not wait to put God's authority first in their lives. If you haven't done so already, don't you wait either.

Discussion Questions

1. How has recognition of God's authority changed the course of nations? America?
2. How do we often unintentionally resist his authority in our personal lives?
3. What would it mean for you to give God authority over your life?

5

What Is Truth?

"What is truth?"

—PONTIUS PILATE (JOHN 18:38)

Is there such a thing as "truth"? These two examples from a former president and prominent news anchor show that a number of influential people still question this idea.

"Implicit . . . in the very idea of ordered liberty . . . is a rejection of absolute truth, the infallibility of any idea or ideology or theology or 'ism', any tyrannical consistency that might lock future generations into a single unalterable course." This quote is from *The Audacity of Hope* by President Obama, written before he was president.[1]

"I think I can be an honest person and lie about any number of things." This is a May 15, 2001 quote from long time news and *60 Minutes* anchor Dan Rather during an interview with Bill O'Reilly.[2]

What is truth? The question Pilate posed to Jesus, and that Jesus had already answered ("I am . . . the Truth" John 14:6) is still being asked. The answer given by philosopher Jean-Paul Sarte is

---

1. Arnn, "Time to give up, or time to fight on?"
2. Noyes, "Clinton's an honest man." 3.

reflective of how it is often being answered and applied to ourselves in today's culture:

"[M]y self is not a stable, solid entity that lasts through time; rather, it is a creation that I must make and remake from moment to moment. Not only must I create myself, but I must also create my world. I do so by bestowing values on the world ... Life has no meaning or value except that which I give to it."[3] The consequences of this belief are manifested in everything from our policies, to our treatment of others and our peace with ourselves.

Why should we care? We should care because even those who deny truth cannot live their lives as though there is no truth. Truth is real. Truth has real consequences. If you don't believe it, step out in front of a car and find out. Denial of truth and tolerance of lies lead to behaviors such as those found in the examples below.

"We routinely wrote scare stories about the hazards of chemicals, employing words like 'cancer,' and 'birth defects' to splash a little cold water in reporters' faces ... We were out to whip the public into a frenzy about the environment." This is a quote from Jim Sibbison, former EPA Press Officer.[4]

"It doesn't matter what is true; it only matters what people believe is true ... You are what the media define you to be. [Greenpeace] became a myth and a myth-generating machine." This was spoken by Paul Watson, founder of the radical environmental organization Greenpeace.[5]

How well does this quote describe our current situation? As Aleksandr Solzhenitsyn wrote, "The permanent lie becomes the only safe form of existence ... There exists a collection of ready-made phrases, a selection of ready-made lies. And not one single speech, nor one single essay or article nor one single book—be it scientific, journalistic, critical, or 'literary,'—can exist without the use of these primary cliches."[6] This is how Solzhenitsyn described the state of political discussion prior to and during the era of Marx,

---

3. Palmer, *Looking at Philosophy*, 372–373.
4. Ray and Guzzo. *Environmental Overkill*, 165.
5. Ray and Guzzo, *Environmental Overkill*, 172.
6. Solzhenitsyn, *The Gulag Archipelago*, Vol. 2, 646.

Lenin, and Stalin that resulted in the killing of at least sixty-five million of their own citizens. We have our own collection of lies and cliches that cannot be contradicted or challenged without risking personal destruction (though not yet physical destruction) through the use of our ready-made labels and lies—"intolerant," "racist," "homophobic," and so forth. This collection even has a name—"political correctness." But what are these cliches based upon?

Conceptions and Outworking of Truth

"What is truth?" Pontius Pilate asked Jesus (John 18:38). He probably asked in a mocking tone. I doubt if he asked because he felt any real curiosity or felt any great desire to find it. He may have. To achieve the position he had reached in a brutal culture of man-centered (as opposed to God-centered) power like in the Roman world, he wouldn't have spent a lot of time concerning himself with "truth." He would have been, as those quoted above, far more concerned with using information—true or otherwise—to influence others to do his bidding, build his base of support, and move up in the hierarchy of power. Anyone so foolish as to put themselves at a disadvantage for the sake of truth was a contemptible knave in his mind, someone who deserved what he got as a result. Does a culture that listens to fake news, believes manufactured crises, and denies biological realities have any greater respect for truth or those who pursue it? Is a society that destroys its connections to the past, such as statues or monuments, and rewrites history one that values truth, or one which merely attempts to attach to itself any vestiges of power that truth still holds?

What is truth—something to align ourselves with, or something to manipulate for our own benefit? Can we truly manipulate it to our own benefit, or not? Is it something we define, control and own, or is it something beyond us that gives us only the illusion of yielding to our power? These are but a few of the questions around truth, and their answers are not merely intellectual exercises. We may be personally faced with some very difficult choices. Do we defend truth and face the consequences, or do we turn a blind eye to its destruction? We have long lived in a nation where many beliefs have been tolerated—even blatantly false ones. The last decade has seen a breathtakingly rapid sea-change in this. It seems everything has been politicized. Today, truth is lost in a "twilight-zone" of surreal political correctness enforced by regulations, law, intense intimidation, and more and more frequently, violence. In the days of the Russian Gulag, a person who tried very hard to stay out of political discussions was taken from his home and led off to be shot. He asked the official, "I know nothing of politics. Why am I to be shot?" The official said, "Because you know nothing of politics, you should be shot." In today's America, staying apolitical is increasingly difficult. With regard to lies, we are entering a time in America where at first we are asked to be "tolerant." Then we are told to "celebrate." Finally, we will be forced to submit. Answers to the question, "What is truth?" are urgently needed.

Many today would say, "If it's true for you, it's true." This is a modern conceit. It is analogous to the expression, "If a tree falls in the woods, does it make a sound?" Of course, when a tree falls it creates sound waves. Those sound waves are heard by animals even if no person is within hearing distance. The idea that a sound can only be made if those sound waves activate a functioning human ear and are communicated to a functioning human mind, is a conceit that ignores the fact that everything has been created and is present to generate a sound recognizable to a receptive and functioning human ear. In an analogous way, truth exists whether or not a human is receptive to it or not. If truth isn't "true to you," it merely means that you don't have ears to hear. You are blocking the successful transmission of truth to heart and mind. But truth still exists.

The understanding of truth from ancient times and across cultures is quite different from the modern concept of "If it's true for you, it's true." As with so many of the slogans that are used to articulate today's shallow, vacuous worldviews, it self-destructs with the slightest challenge. "If it's true for you, it's true" sounds very open-minded and inclusive—which are ideals placed high on today's ideological altar—but it is actually a closed-minded exclusive truth claim. It's a black and white all-inclusive assertion that there are no absolute truths. It is also an arrogant assertion that any and all of us can claim to know and own truth, no matter how superficially or insincerely we search for it. It trivializes truth, mocks it. Consider Figure 5.1, which I call the Circles of Living.

Circles of Living

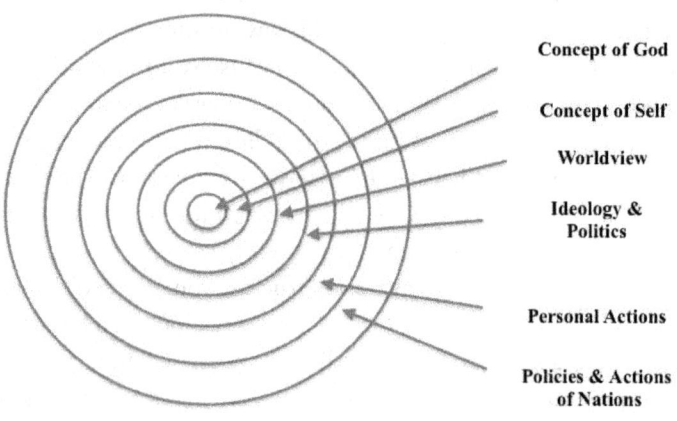

Figure 5.1 Circles of Living

This figure illustrates the fact that our collective actions as nations and our personal actions as individuals spring from our core understanding of God: his existence, his character, and his relationship to us. We spend the majority of our reflection and activity in the outer circles without questioning the inner core upon which our most visible exterior lives are based. Think about each of these circles, beginning with your concept of God. Does he exist? Does he take a personal interest in me? Am I made in his image? What purpose does he have for me in this life? Is this life all there is? And so on. The working out of all the other Circles of Living based on fundamentally different core concepts of God is what we see in our highly polarized, politicized and increasingly autocratic society.

What Is Truth?

In his great little book *Tactics: A Game Plan for Discussing Christian Convictions*, Greg Koukl asks, "Are moral laws the product of chance? If so, why obey them? . . . The concept of moral obligation [outer circle of Personal Actions] is unintelligible apart from the idea of God . . . To say that something is evil [or hypocritical, unjust, etc.] is to say it is not the way it is supposed to be. This makes no sense unless things are supposed to be different. Yet this is precisely what the relativist denies."[7] The relativist attempts the impossible—to live a moral life, which is to say, one that transcends self, yet denies any transcendent basis for morality.

In his classic book *The Screwtape Letters*, C.S. Lewis has a mentor demon, Screwtape, teaching a student demon through a series of letters. He uses a concept similar to the Circles of Living. Screwtape says, "Do what you will, there is going to be some benevolence, as well as some malice, in your patient's soul [Humans are these demons' patients]. The great thing is to direct the malice to his immediate neighbors whom he meets every day and to thrust his benevolence out to the remote circumference, to people he does not know."[8] Think about this. The great "silent majority" of people are hard-working, responsible, mostly God-fearing, and have traditional values. These are the people you meet every day and they are being characterized as closed-minded haters. There is a concerted attempt to direct malice at them. We only occasionally meet those who are incensed by "micro-aggressions" and bizarre interpretations of facts because they are so few, though loud. However they are held up to us as heroes. The attempt is to have our benevolence directed to them. The desired outcome is what we see happening today as American society is fragmented into special-interest groups based on race, gender, and social status and pitted against each other by petty, outdated, or imagined offenses. Lewis' demons were well-aware of these tactics and described them quite well: "The malice thus becomes wholly real and the benevolence largely imaginary. There is no good at all in inflaming his hatred of Germans [The enemy during World War II] if, at the same time,

---

7. Koukl, *Tactics*, 134–137.
8. Lewis, *Screwtape Letters*, 28.

a pernicious habit of charity is growing up between him and his mother, his employer, and the man he meets in the train."

Then, as in the Circles of Living, the demons explain how critical the core is to the outcome they desire from their "patients." For the Christian, the core of their being is Christ. For the atheist or relativist, their core is completely ambiguous and empty. Hence, their external lives are facades and fantasies—fertile fields for all kinds of evil.

> "Think of your man as a series of concentric circles, his will being the innermost, his intellect coming next, and finally his fantasy. You can hardly hope, at once, to exclude from all the circles everything that smells of the Enemy [God]: but you must keep on shoving all the virtues [real virtues] outward till they are finally located in the circle of fantasy, and all the desirable qualities [desirable to demons] inward into the Will. It is only in so far as they reach the Will and are there embodied in habits that the virtues [real virtues] are really fatal to us."9

What Lewis describes through his demons is what is actually being done today, particularly by the political left. The empty, vacuous slogans of "benevolence" are in the outer Circles of Living in public action and ideology and politics—"coexist," "give peace a chance," "stop the hate," and so forth. In C.S. Lewis' circles this "benevolence" exists far out in the circle of fantasy. When I was on the executive team of a large company I remember sitting at a banquet for an institute at a large state university, which we funded with many millions of dollars. A young scientist at my table said she only did work that had an impact beginning at least five hundred years into the future. I was stunned! This "benevolence" is fantasy. In the name of this imaginary future "benevolence" all kinds of real evils are justified today, in the real, here-and-now world. Heinrich Himmler[10] understood this well. He recruited his SS-men from

---

9. Ibid., 28.

10. Heinrich Himmler was one of the most powerful men in Nazi Germany. He was the head of the ruthless SS, Hitler's secret police.

What Is Truth?

people who weren't interested in "everyday problems" but only in "ideological questions of importance for decades and centuries."[11]

Lewis' concentric circles and the Circles of Living are similar in that both show how core beliefs hold the key to how we live our lives as individuals and nations. As core beliefs about the Circles of Living shift, this leads to shifts in policies and actions of nations. Harvard professor Juan Enriquez pointed out that 75 percent of nations represented at the United Nations had not existed only fifty years prior.[12] Nations are rising and falling at a rapid rate due to their policies and actions. Public opinion changes, but truth is unchangeable. Now consider Figure 5.2.

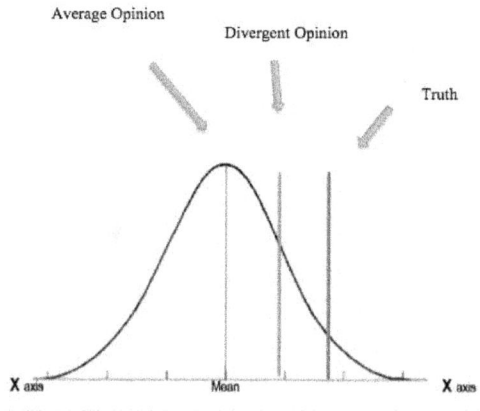

Figure 5.2 Fallacy of the Righteous Average: As Divergent Opinion moves closer to Average Opinion, it (in some instances, as the one illustrated) moves *farther* from the Truth.

Notice the location of the lines for truth, average public opinion, and public opinion diverging from the average. We hear a lot about "extreme left" or "extreme right" politically. The implication is that the truth lies between and we should strive for the middle.

11. Arendt, *The Origins of Totalitarianism*, 420.
12. Enriquez, *As the Future Catches You*, 15.

This ignores where truth actually lies. Truth may actually lie farther from the middle of opinions. As the divergent opinion moves closer to the average, it actually moves farther from the truth—at least in some cases.

The Fallacy of the Righteous Average is the phrase I use to describe the idea that those far from the mean of opinion are also far from the truth. Discussions about "extreme right" or "extreme left" politically have no inherent claim to where truth lies and are only concerned with influencing *opinions*. Healthy societies focus on discussions around what is or isn't *true*, not merely opinions. If you want to influence any of the outer Circles of Living and move your brothers and sisters, friends, neighbors and countrymen closer to the truth, you must ultimately influence their concept of God. This is why evangelism is so essential, and why prayer in schools and Christianity generally is under attack. Enemies of truth also understand this and resist with all their might.

God Is Truth

What does the Bible tells us about truth? It tells us that God is a God of truth: "Into your hands I commit my spirit; redeem me, O Lord, the God of truth" (Ps 31:5). "God is not a man, that he should lie" (Num 23:19). "It is impossible for God to lie" (Heb 6:18). It also tells us that we would fall away from the truth and turn to lies: "[T]hey exchanged the truth about God for a lie" (Rom 1:25). Though we should hardly need to be reminded of that; lies are all around us, as my examples at the beginning of this chapter illustrate. Our eagerness to listen to and act on lies is traced all the way back to the Garden of Eden. But God didn't leave us without hope, to remain dead in lies, lost from the truth. Jesus is the way and the truth and the life (John 14:6). The statement prompting the question from Pilate, "What is truth?" was the result of Jesus explaining the way of salvation even to his executioner, saying, "[F]or this reason I was born, and for this I came into the world, to testify to the truth. Everyone on the side of truth listens to me" (John 18:37). He promises us, "I will not leave you orphans; I will come to you" (John 14:18); "And I will ask the Father, and he will give you another Helper, to be with you forever, even the Spirit of Truth, whom the world cannot receive, because it neither sees him nor knows him." (John 14:16–17); "When the Spirit comes, he will guide you into all truth" (John 16:13). And truth is to be used as a "belt of armor" against the spiritual forces of evil that we face (Eph 6:14). "We cannot do anything against the truth" (2 Cor 13:8). So truth is not something we ultimately manipulate. We must align with it. This is because truth is as Webster's 1828 Dictionary defines it: "Conformity to fact or reality; exact accordance with that which is, or has been, or shall be. We rely on the truth of scriptural prophecies."[13] But perhaps most importantly, God himself is truth. Jesus speaking to the Father in John 17:17 says, "Your word is truth." The Greek word here is not an adjective,—*true*, but a noun—*truth*. What is being communicated is not that God's word conforms to some standard of truth, but that it is truth itself. It is the standard against which everything else must be compared. God is truth.

Therefore, it logically flows that a life committed to God, and God's Word, Jesus Christ, is a life that seeks to live in alignment with the truth. It is a life that strives to be authentic and true to self because it has purpose and meaning that transcends self. It is a life that has dignity, regardless of circumstances. It is a life that enjoys inner peace because at its core is the peace of Christ.

Discussion Questions

Comment on: "If opinions vary from extreme left to extreme right, shouldn't we move our thinking closer to the middle to find the truth?"

Comment on: "Absolute truth is intolerant. We should honor each individual's personal truth."

---

13. Webster, *An American Dictionary of the English Language.*

6

The Tyranny of Good Intentions

"O foolish Galatians! Who has bewitched you? . . . Having begun by the Spirit, are you now being perfected by the flesh?"

—GAL 3:1-3

THINK OF THE LAST time something turned out really badly for you and you were told to not get too upset because the person who did it had good intentions. Did you soften your anger or negative reaction? You probably did. Most of us take into account whether or not someone intended to do us harm because we all know that nobody's perfect. If we treat the other person with kindness when they try to do something good for us and it doesn't work out, perhaps they will return the favor if someday we fail in attempting to do them a good turn. This may or may not be a good assumption.

Intentions spring from our worldview, which depends on our answer to the question, "Is there a God?" From the answer to this question flow many other questions, such as "What kind of God is he?" and "What does he expect of me?" If our answer is that there isn't a God, our questions will be different. Since in this worldview there is nothing greater than the world, and no future life beyond this one, we may ask, "How can I get all I can while I can?" Or, since there is no God to give meaning or purpose when we see pain and suffering, we would ask, "What difference does it make?" Our worldview, our life, and our intentions in life are shaped by our answer to the question "Is there a God?" Intentions have intent—purpose; they direct our actions. Our actions are responses to God's grace—even if we don't believe in God.

In *The Cost of Discipleship*, Pastor Dietrich Bonhoeffer contrasted "costly grace" with "cheap grace."[1] I will add a third, "despised grace." In reality, these categories don't describe grace, but rather our *response* to grace. God's grace doesn't change. We will look at each of these individually with a view toward how our intentions are formed from these responses to grace. But first, one might ask, "What is grace?"

What Is Grace?

"Grace" is used in a variety of ways in the Bible. Typically, "grace" is used to mean divine favor or goodwill and its expression in favors and blessings from God. It is an attribute of God. Berkhof defines it as "God's free, sovereign, undeserved favor or love to man, in his state of sin and guilt, which manifests itself in the forgiveness of sin and deliverance from its penalty. It is connected with the mercy of God as distinguished from his justice."[2] For those unaccustomed to thinking in terms of spiritual things, "grace" includes spiritual blessings. They are expressed not merely, or even primarily, in our comfort and happiness in this earthly life. It is used in the sense of spiritual renewal from our sinful, fallen state, and redemption of our status before a righteous God so that we are forgiven of our sins through faith in Jesus Christ. "For the grace of God hath appeared, bringing salvation to all men" (Titus 2:11).[3] So what did Bonhoeffer mean by "costly grace" and "cheap grace"?

1. Bonhoeffer, *Cost of Discipleship*, 43–56.
2. Berkhoff, *Systematic Theology*, 426–446.
3. This should not be interpreted as an argument that all will be saved and go to heaven. It is abundantly clear from Scripture that only the elect will be saved from eternal damnation. But this is a topic for another place.

Costly Grace

Bonhoeffer says, "When Christ calls a man, he bids him come and die."[4] This is true. But it is only half true. With our orientation on our present earthly life, this is what we often focus on the most. However, the more important half of the truth speaks of our eternal life; when Christ calls a man, he bids him come and live! This truth isn't transient as is the first half. And the life promised isn't one in a fallen world. It is a life spent in the fullness, joy and perfection of heaven! Costly grace is a costly investment. In it we invest our time, our social status, our resources, our life—everything. It is a tangible reflection of the depth and sincerity of our faith in Christ and his promises. In our willingness to pursue costly grace we know our rewards in heaven far outweigh our investment. "[T]he kingdom of heaven is like a merchant in search of fine pearls, who, on finding one pearl of great value, went and sold all that he had and bought it" (Matt 13:45–46).

"Costly grace" might better be named "priceless grace." Those who pursue costly grace seek the eternal things of Christ. They know that the "good" in true "good intentions" comes only from him because he is the source of all that is good. The intent, or purpose, in these intentions is to be obedient to him, no matter the personal cost. There can be no "tyranny" in these intentions because they are not in service of self, nor are they interested in the submission of others. As Christ set the example for us to follow in serving others (John 13:12–17), true good intentions are those that benefit others.

Cheap Grace

Bonhoeffer contrasts cheap grace with costly grace:

> "Cheap grace is the deadly enemy of our Church... Cheap grace means grace sold on the market like cheapjacks' wares ... Grace without price; grace without cost! The essence of grace, we suppose, is that the account has been

---

4. Bonhoeffer, *Cost of Discipleship*, 11.

paid in advance; and because it has been paid, everything can be had for nothing. Since the cost was infinite, the possibilities of using and spending it are infinite. What would grace be if it were not cheap?"[5]

There are certainly elements of this that a good Reformed theologian would agree with. The price *was* paid in advance. By God's grace, Christ paid for our sins—once for all—on the cross of Calvary. In that sense, everything can be had for nothing. But using that to do what we please would be willfully missing the point. The point Bonhoeffer is making is the same one that Paul sarcastically raised, then immediately shot down. "What shall we say then? Are we to continue in sin that grace may abound? By no means! How can we who died to sin still live in it?" (Rom 6:1–2). Bonhoeffer is criticizing our hearts hardened against God's grace and our lack of obedience to him.

He goes on: "Cheap grace means grace as a doctrine, a principle, a system. It means forgiveness of sins proclaimed as a general truth, the love of God taught as the Christian 'conception' of God. An intellectual assent to that idea is held to be of itself sufficient to secure remission of sins; no contrition is required." Cheap grace still makes a show of belief in God, but it isn't serious or sincere because it redefines the plain teaching of Scripture to mean something that costs little or nothing. Where costly grace requires a costly investment of our time, social status, resources, and may even place our life at risk; cheap grace attempts to have it both ways by responding to God's grace, but on man's terms. Man attempts to define what is "good" apart from God. We see this in churches teaching the "prosperity gospel," or liberal churches' focus on a "social justice gospel." The prosperity gospel teaches the idea that God wants us to be rich, famous, powerful, and successful according to man's measures of success. The social justice gospel focuses on addressing social problems—real or imagined—and doing so with man's solutions under a thin veneer of "God-talk" to provide an aura of higher purpose. Because man's solutions boil down to solutions from a few men who think they know what's best for everyone else, there is a

5. Bonhoeffer, *Cost of Discipleship*, 43.

very strong influence from ideologies that centralize authority and power into the hands of a few elites via the State. The influence of these ideologies explains why these churches are liberal and leftist politically. Their intent (purpose) aligns with the intent of Marxism, communism, socialism and humanism. They all seek man-made solutions through obedience to the State, rather than God. They, not God, define what is good. They practice a tyranny of good intentions, which I will describe in a moment.

Despised Grace

Bonhoeffer included only two contrasting categories of grace because he was making a point about the state of Christianity as it was practiced in the early and mid-1900s. I am not only considering Christians in this book, so I add a third response to God's grace. Despised grace is a response to God's grace that denies its very existence because it denies God's existence. In contrast to those who seek costly grace, those who live according to despised grace seek the transient things of man. They believe, as Sarte wrote, "Life has no meaning or value except that which I give to it."[6] But this pathetic belief is essentially no different than the child's belief that if they close their eyes no one will see them. Telling yourself that your life has the meaning you give it doesn't make it true. For intelligent adults to hold such a belief, as many millions do in God-denying ideologies such as Marxism, communism and humanism, it must be willful. As we saw in chapter 2, this willful rebellion against God's authority was anticipated as a consequence of the Fall when God put enmity between the seed of the woman (those who place their faith in God) and the seed of the serpent (those who rebel against God).

This willful self-delusion is a desperate place to be. The world of those who hold this view crumbles when they are forced to face the truth. Sarte was among the most influential philosophers of the twentieth century, he articulated the fearful dilemma of those

---

6. Palmer, *Looking at Philosophy*, 372–373.

who hold this worldview: "[M]y self is not a stable, solid entity that lasts through time; rather, it is a creation that I must make and remake from moment to moment. Not only must I create myself, but I must also create my world. I do so by bestowing values on the world." What if the world rejects his values? His delusion is shattered, and his self along with it. He is left with nothing—no meaning, no purpose and the creation he labored moment to moment to make, is exposed as a hideous lie.

Those who despise God's grace have much to lose; they lose everything if they are unable to "bestow their values on the world." They *must* make the world accept their values, and the world must accept their values as good. "Good intentions" in their worldview are those which result in the acceptance of their values by others. They demand obedience to their values, not obedience to God, and desperately create tyranny in these "good" intentions through the submission of others to their will.

Exposing the Tyranny of Good Intentions

As we saw in the fallacy of the righteous average, holding a belief in common with others is irrelevant to its truth. If we hold a common belief in what is "good," we may share the same intentions. But sharing the same intentions or having opposing intentions is immaterial for whether or not the purpose of our intentions is the right one. Adolf Hitler and his millions of supporters in the Nazi party held many of the same intentions. Most people today now recognize that they were not the right intentions. The basis of intentions is what determines their right-ness, or in Christian language, their righteousness. As we saw in the last chapter, how we know what is true, that is, the assumptions which form a reliable basis for our intentions, can only be based on God. No other basis transcends the limited and flawed opinions of man. When man apart from God determines the intended purpose for anything of importance, and consequently who is forced to live with it, it should be no surprise that the people who benefit are those with the power to dictate which intentions are "good" and worth pursuing. These "good intentions are used to mask the will to power, creating a "tyranny of good intentions."

Jesus repeatedly confronted the Pharisees for the burdens they placed on others but personally ignored: "Jesus said to the crowds and his disciples, 'The scribes and Pharisees... preach, but do not practice. They tie up heavy burdens, hard to bear, and lay them on people's shoulders, but they themselves are not willing to move them with their finger. They do all their deeds to be seen by others... they love the place of honor... the best seats in the synagogues... greetings in the marketplaces and being called 'rabbi' by others'" (Matt 23:1–7). They conducted their tyranny under the pretense of good intentions, of worshipping God. Jesus told them, "Woe to you, scribes and Pharisees, hypocrites! For you are like whitewashed tombs, which outwardly appear beautiful, but within are full of dead people's bones and all uncleanness. So you also outwardly appear righteous to others, but within you are full of hypocrisy and lawlessness" (Matt 23:27–28). Their true intent resulted not in worshipping God, as they wanted people to believe, but in demanding the crucifixion of God incarnate, Jesus Christ.

We are no different today. Last winter I was in Switzerland attending one of those navel-gazing leadership workshops where corporations send their up-and-comers (or perhaps in my case, their has-beens) to learn their personality profiles and gain insights into how that affects their effectiveness as leaders. One of those assigned to my team for the workshop was a young Swiss woman named Corrine, who frequently began statements with what she clearly felt was an admirable intention, "I'm not judging, I'm just curious" while listening to answers with which she disagreed with a detached and slightly amused look, as an anthropologist who was taking field notes on a newly-discovered sub-species of *Homo sapiens* that could potentially help her bridge the evolutionary gap from ape to her highly advanced, civilized pinnacle of humanity.

One day we shared our life's journeys as one of our group exercises. Our assignment was to take a sheet of flip chart paper and draw out the significant milestones of our life's journey and share with each other how they influenced our leadership approaches.

Though the youngest by many years, Corrine's life's journey required two full sheets, at least in her mind. It was an all too common story in today's world dominated by progressive ideology—a family that was loosely held together and finally broke; a mother who was immersed in progressive ideology; a father who failed as a husband and later as a father—"but was not judgmental"; a heroin-addicted brother who spent much of his life in prison—"but didn't judge others." Corrine proudly explained to us how she had experimented with all religions, with drugs, with sex. She clearly felt that all this experimentation had given her more wisdom at her young age than any of us old fuddy-duddies. She liked pointing out that she was now "husband" to a woman, perhaps to gauge its shock value or to surface those who might make a *judgment* as to what effect such an arrangement might have on their two sons.

As is so often the case, she was very judgmental in her non-judgmentalism. The lessons and knowledge of countless generations before her meant nothing. Traditions were seen as biases and superstitions of outdated worldviews and superstitious belief in God rather than accumulated knowledge that has withstood generations of testing and challenges, and the commands of a true and living God. I don't know if she had ever heard of Jean-Paul Sarte, but she was a zealot of his grace-despising worldview: "Not only must I create myself, but I must also create my world. I do so by bestowing values on the world." Because of this, judgment could only be applied to those who don't hold her views. She remained completely oblivious to the irony. But Corrine is not unique. Just consider a few of the following "enlightened" views that we are being asked to put in place and the "beautiful" things they bring, if only we Christians would come around to this way of thinking. Not all of these views are directly linked to Biblical teachings and some sincere Bible-believing Christians may disagree with this assessment of them, but all in one way or another are aimed at undermining God's sovereignty.

- Feminism: Because women must be freed from the oppression of men

- Gender "self-identification": Because biological gender is limiting
- Secularism: Because religion is hypocritical and oppressive
- Human-caused climate change: Because we can control the global climate in a similar way to raising or lowering temperatures in our own living room
- Homosexuality: Because people should be able to love whoever they want
- Tolerance : Because intolerance is for racists and bigots
- Socialism and communism: Because capitalism is unfair
- Non-judgmentalism: Because being judgmental closes us off from the other and even Jesus said, "Judge not lest ye be judged"

These are but a small sampling. If we ignore the underlying political agendas in these and simply take them at face value, as many people do, how can a sincere, well-intentioned soul seeking penance from their "wrongs" navigate this jungle of offenses, slights, insults and oppression? If you happen to have been born white, your very existence is a privilege that you must somehow atone for. But don't think your hands are clean if you're a minority. Oh no! If you believe marriage is only between a man and a woman, you're a "sinner." Do you get compensated well for doing better work than others? That's unfair! Your earnings must be taken away. In his book *The Gulag Archipelago*, Aleksandr Solzhenitsyn said, "To do evil a human being must first of all believe that what he's doing is good... Fortunately, it is in the nature of the human being to seek a justification for his actions."[7] Living in a concentration camp (*gulag*), he knew firsthand the logical result of this tyranny of good intentions that justified the very existence of the gulags.

He continued by saying, "Shakespeare's evildoers stopped short at a dozen corpses because they had no ideology. Ideology— that is what gives evildoing its long-sought justification and gives the evildoer the necessary steadfastness and determination. That is

---

7. Solzhenitsyn, *Gulag Archipelago*, Vol. 1, 173–174.

the social theory which helps to make his acts seem good instead of bad in his own and others' eyes, so that he won't hear reproaches and curses but will receive praise and honors." What he's getting at is that if you want to carry out evil on a large scale, turning from God's authority to man's as a society, you must cloak it within an ideology known by its nice-sounding intentions. Looking at outcomes won't do. Outcomes are real. Ideologies are theories. If you ignore the politics of the nice-sounding intentions we are confronted with today (which you really shouldn't), the best that can be said is that we live under a tyranny of good intentions. With all the agitation for tolerance and the outrage against oppression of all kinds (except against Christians, of course), we should be witnessing the dawn of a utopia of peace and love. The lion should be lying down with the lamb by now. Christianity should be thoroughly discredited as an outmoded relic. The reality is the exact opposite!

Christian Life Under the Tyranny

Despised grace is on the march in Western society. We Christians will be tested, many even persecuted for our beliefs. Our intentions will be questioned, maligned and impugned, while those of the Enemy will be held up as kind, honorable, just and enlightened. Jesus prayed to the Father not that we be taken from this fallen world, but that we be protected from the evil one (John 17:15). Being protected from the evil one doesn't mean we are to be isolated from him, as if that were possible in this world. Since its founding until the last generation, America has been a relative oasis from both the "hot" persecution of Christians, physical violence against Christians for their faith or lack of protection for their rights as citizens, and the even more pernicious "cold" persecution. For at least a few generations now the greater threat in the Western world has been "cold" persecution, the discrediting or belittling of Christians and their beliefs. If you doubt the damage that this has done, take a trip to western Europe and count the number of churches that are empty or have been converted to restaurants, theaters, and even bars. The unspoken contract that has been made with Satan is, "Let us live nice, comfortable lives and we will renounce Christ." It is a similar offer to that which Satan made to Jesus during his temptation in the wilderness: "All these [kingdoms] will I give you, if you will fall down and worship me" (Matt 4:9). It has been slowly poisoning our churches and our society in America, too.

The first signs are the corruption of costly grace into cheap grace. Mainline Christian denomination membership has been in free-fall since the mid-1960s. The United Methodist Church (UMC), for example, has lost members every year since 1965.[8] If you had a company with that disastrous a record with your customers, you would make dramatic changes. Yet the UMC as well as the other liberal churches have doubled down on their determination to turn from Jesus' clear teachings and commands towards what could be characterized as salvation by social justice. The United Church of Christ lost 53 percent of its members—over a million during roughly the same time period.[9] The Episcopal Church has had similar losses to those of the UCC, including over 1.6 million members.[10] And the PCUSA (Presbyterian Church of the USA) has *never* had an increase in membership since it was formed in 1983. The last recorded membership gain in its two predecessor denominations was in 1965.[11] On the other hand, the

---

8. This information is from a January 29, 2015 posting. Woodward, "United Methodist decline due to liberal theology takeover."

9. This data from the United Church of Christ's own data was during the period 1964-2014. Center for Research, Analytics and Data, "Statistical Profile, Fall 2014," uccfiles.com.

10. The Episcopal Church in the U.S. lost 47 percent of its members from 1960 through 2014, from 3,444,000 in 1960 to 1,817,004 in 2014. The data used in these calculations came from the World Almanac and Yearbook of American Churches. Wendell Cox Consultancy, "Trends in Large US Church Membership from 1960," www.demographia.com.

Another posting, this one from October 9, 2015, not only showed the shocking loss of membership in the Episcopalian Church in the United States. It also showed an astonishing lack of introspection as to the reasons for the losses by church leadership. Walton, "Episcopalians continue bleeding members, attendance at alarming rate." https://juicyecumenism.com.

11. This is from a May 13, 2015 posting. Kinkaid, "PCUSA continues membership decline—92,433 members gone in 2014," www.layman.org.

denominations that have been growing are the conservative ones. The Presbyterian Church of America (PCA) membership is up about 5 percent in the last five years alone.[12] Pentecostal denominations are growing even faster.[13] The distinctions between the seed of the serpent and the seed of the woman are becoming more starkly defined. Membership in liberal "Christian" denominations provided a camouflage for those seeking cheap grace during those periods in society when being a Christian still conferred benefits. As those benefits become disadvantages, we see the shakeout in liberal church membership.

In chapters 3 and 4 we discussed the importance of recognizing God's authority in our lives and being obedient to him. Several chapters have addressed truth and the need to follow God's truth. By turning from God to man's itching ears, the liberal churches are now reaping what they have sown. It is a seductive path following man-derived intentions that sound so good. Pursuing costly grace means we must stay alert to what is happening outside of our church bubble and test the spirits that surround us in society (1 John 4:1). We must be the watchmen for our brothers and sisters, friends, neighbors and family. We are to be obedient to Christ in this fallen world. So when we are asked to change our views to nice-sounding more enlightened views we should test the spirits from which they come.

For example, consider one view that Corrine was very fond of: being non-judgmental. We Christians are said to be very judgmental and this makes us bad, according to the enlightened, "progressive" view.

The word *judge* means, "To discern; to distinguish; to consider accurately for the purpose of forming an opinion or conclusion."[14]

---

12. These data include the years 2012 through 2016. Administrative Committee PCA, "PCA statistics: Five-year summary," www.pcaac.org.

13. For example, Assemblies of God reported their 27th consecutive year of growth in 2016, reaching over 1.8 million members. And, they are growing at a rate of over 50 percent above the U.S. population growth rate. Bradford, "Report of the General Secretary, Assemblies of God," www.ag.org.

14. Webster, *Dictionary of the English Language*.

Is it "non-judgmental" to *judge* harmful behavior as acceptable? Why do we judge it good to provide needles to a heroin addict so they can "safely" shoot poison into their arms in a city park, as Corrine's brother did, yet judge it bad to provide him with Scripture? How did we get to a point in which becoming accomplice to slow suicide from drug addiction is considered non-judgmental and therefore good, while helping a person to confront a problem—or even calling it a problem—crosses a taboo line of passing judgment? The outcome of these "good" intentions in reality harms those they claim to be concerned for. They also harm those who are in fact doing the difficult job of working to help those with self-destructive behaviors.

Christians are often reminded by non-Christians and liberal Christians that the Bible says, "Do not judge, or you too will be judged... Why do you look at the speck of sawdust in your brother's eye and pay no attention to the plank in your own eye?... You hypocrite, first take the plank out of your own eye, and then you will see clearly to remove the speck from your brother's eye" (Matt 7:1–5). But the Bible also says, "Stop judging by mere appearances, and make a right judgment" (John 7:24) and, "Why don't you judge for yourselves what is right?" (Luke 12:57). When we are faced with statements from the Bible that sound contradictory, we simply haven't looked deeply enough into what we are being told. Test the spirits behind what we are being led to believe when people assert certain parts of Scripture and ignore other parts.

Setting the Captives Free

Let's step back and take a broader look at what's going on. When Jesus was talking to Pontius Pilate he said, "For this purpose I was born and came into the world—to bear witness to the truth" (John 18:37). This is a very instructive statement! He didn't say he came into the world merely to *tell* the truth. Jesus said he came into the world to *bear witness* to the truth. Why does he use this courtroom language? Because truth is on trial. There are two opposing sides in a trial; in the cosmic battle, the Father of Lies is opposing the Truth, the Way and the Life, Jesus Christ. While truth is on trial, deceit is lurking, crouching like a lion, seeking to take us captive (1 Pet 5:8).

Colossians 2:8 says, "See to it that no one takes you *captive* by philosophy and empty deceit, according to human tradition, according to the elemental spirits of the world, and not according to Christ" (italics mine). Using an imaginary conversation between an elder demon, Screwtape, and his student demon, Wormwood, C.S. Lewis provides a very insightful comment on being taken captive by philosophy and empty deceit according to human tradition. Screwtape, the older demon, tells Wormwood, "Leave it to them [humans] to discuss whether 'Love,' or 'patriotism,' or 'celibacy,' or candles on altars, or teetotalism, or education, are 'good' or 'bad.' Can't you see there is no answer? Nothing matters at all except the tendency of a given state of mind, in given circumstances, to move a particular patient [human] at a particular moment nearer to the Enemy [God] or nearer to us."[15] Lewis is saying what really matters is our faith in Jesus Christ and our obedience to him. He is in control. Everything else is a distraction.

How can we apply this? Firstly, we truly must be very alert to what is happening. What seem like well-intended efforts often are anything but that. Think of the list I gave above. Satan uses these nice-sounding intentions not merely to mislead us, but to take us *captive* by moving us little by little closer to him and his snares. And who are the captives? They are those opposed to God. They live under the tyranny of man-defined good intentions and are trying to impose them on Christians. Whether you were an Ammonite worshipping Molech, giving your son or daughter to be burned alive with the "good intention" of satisfying Molech (Jer 32:35), or you are a modern-day Marxist chipping away at your country's Christian foundations and condemning your sons and daughters to your socialist "utopia," you are building your godless tyranny on good intentions. Lenin had a name for those who believe these good intentions—a rather harsh one, "useful idiots," because they were useful to him in advancing his godless tyranny. As Christians we have a different name for them: captives. We should

---

15. Lewis, *Screwtape Letters*, 101–102.

feel Christian compassion for them, while not naively giving in and becoming ensnared ourselves. They need Jesus. Jesus came to set the captives free (Isa 61:1; Luke 4:18).

Think of the very public dispute that took place when the apostle Paul confronted Peter to his face (Gal 2:15–16). Peter was slipping back into the man-defined, well-intentioned practices of following food restrictions and not mixing with Gentiles. Out of fear, he let down his guard and began following the practices of the "religious" Jews from Jerusalem, the circumcision party. Most people at that time would have at least said that these Jews had good intentions, but Paul instantly recognized the danger and brought Peter to his senses. If Peter could fall for what man holds to be good intentions, so can you and I. Remember what Jesus told the rich young man, "There is only one who is good" (Matt 19:17). Remember also the words of John,

> "Beloved, do not believe every spirit, but test the spirits to see whether they are from God, for many false prophets have gone into the world. By this you know the Spirit of God: every spirit that confesses that Jesus Christ has come in the flesh is from God, and every spirit that does not confess Jesus is not from God. This is the spirit of the antichrist, which you heard was coming and now is in the world already . . . They are from the world; therefore they speak from the world, and the world listens to them. We are from God. Whoever knows God listens to us [John and the apostles]; whoever is not from God does not listen to us. By this we know the Spirit of truth and the spirit of error" (1 John 4:1–6).

Discussion Questions

1. What does the phrase "tyranny of good intentions" mean?
2. How does this tyranny affect Christians? How should we respond?

7

Postmodernism and Power

"Truth is nowhere to be found, and whoever shuns evil becomes a prey"

—ISA 59:16

The Hopelessness of Postmodernism

RAVI ZACHARIAS, A FAMOUS Christian writer, evangelist, and apologist, tells a story of an encounter he had at a question and answer session after one of his speeches:

> "At one of my lectures on 'Man's Search for Meaning,' a student rose to his feet and shouted, 'Ah, everything in life is meaningless.' I insisted that he could not possibly believe that. With an equally intense retort he countered that he did. This repetitive exchange went back and forth a few times. Then not wanting to exacerbate the young man's frustration and having planned for a safe departure from campus, I decided to bring the discussion to an end. I asked him if he thought his statement was a meaningful one. There was an acute silence, and then he hesitantly answered, 'Yes.' I only had to add that if his assertion was meaningful, then everything in life was not meaningless.

If, on the other hand, everything was indeed meaningless, his assertion was meaningless too, and, therefore, in effect, he had said nothing."[1]

The contention that absolute truth doesn't exist is so easily destroyed it's like shooting fish in a barrel. Philosophers have spent their whole lives pondering this student's assertion that Ravi destroyed in less than five minutes. So how can gibberish, utter nonsense, carry such influence over us? Why does it not die quickly as it should?

We Christians know the answer to this because we understand the reality of God and Satan. God's Word gives us the more comprehensive understanding that non-Christians lack, so we clearly see the answer in the ongoing spiritual warfare of this world. But what about non-believers? Postmodernism is probably the greatest influence on the worldview of non-believers. What is postmodernism and what are the consequences for non-believers, for Christians, and for society?

In this chapter I make frequent reference to *The Origins of Totalitarianism* by Hannah Arendt. She was a Holocaust survivor and her book explains the conditions under which totalitarianism arises. Postmodernism, atheism, and totalitarianism are simply three faces of the same evil in that they all deny God. What Jesus said in John 8:42–47 applies to those denying God: "If God were your father, you would love me . . . You are of your father the devil, and your will is to do your father's desires . . . Whoever is of God hears the words of God. The reason why you do not hear them is that you are not of God."

༄

The worldview of those denying absolute truth is perhaps best captured by Shakespeare's *Macbeth*,

> *"Out, out brief candle!*
> *Life's but a walking shadow, a poor player*
> *That struts and frets his hour upon the stage*

---

1. Zacharias, *Real Face of Atheism*, 73–74.

And then is heard no more; it is a tale
Told by an idiot, full of sound and fury,
Signifying nothing."[2]

It's a statement of meaninglessness, hopelessness, purposelessness. It voices the utter emptiness of someone who realizes they have nothing, are nothing and have no hope of this ever changing. It's precisely what drives many to seek meaning in activist causes or power over others in a desperate attempt to counter the powerlessness they feel without Christ. As I mentioned in chapter 2, Heinrich Himmler, the head of Adolf Hitler's secret police, understood this well; he recruited his sadistic SS men from people who weren't interested in everyday problems but only in "ideological questions of importance for decades and centuries," or as Hannah Arendt put it, those with a "passionate inclination toward the most abstract notions as guides for life, and the general contempt for even the most obvious rules of common sense."[3] This contempt for traditions, traditional values, and Christianity in particular, is alive and well today. How does postmodernism in its various forms manifest itself in modern culture and what are the dangers it poses for society and for our souls?

The Will to Power

The worldview captured in *Macbeth* is a form of nihilism, the belief that all values are baseless and nothing can be known or communicated. There are various names and flavors of this same basic idea: relativism, postmodernism, atheism, deconstructionism, and existentialism.[4] They have been the cool, edgy, non-conformist

2. Shakespeare, *Complete Works of William Shakespeare. (Macbeth),* 1068. Act 5, Scene 5.

3. Arendt, *Origins of Totalitarianism,* 420.

4. Pluralism could also be included in this list. While it superficially claims belief that all main religions lead to the same deity, by this same claim it denies the fundamentally contradictory truth claims made by these religions. In effect pluralism, as nihilism, denies the validity of the foundational bases of these religions therefore the bases of the values they espouse.

worldview of artists, revolutionaries, intellectuals, anarchists, and radicals for centuries. In fact, Saul Alinsky, the communist, community organizer of the 1930s whom Barack Obama and Hillary Clinton both studied before they rose to national prominence,[5] and whose tactics Obama taught,[6,7] dedicated his book *Rules for Radicals* to that nihilist that he called "the first radical," none other than Lucifer, otherwise known as Satan.[8] People are still being trained today in his techniques at the Industrial Areas Foundation in Chicago (www.industrialareasfoundation.org). And when a riot pops up, whether in Ferguson, Baltimore, or Charlotte, it almost always connects back to this organization.[9]

Although nihilism has often been the ideology of the "cool" and trendy, it is a supremely gloomy outlook, which explains much of the self-destructive behavior that we see in celebrities like Harvey Weinstein. In recognition of this, some nihilists like Karen Carr try to put a happy face on it by what she calls "cheerful nihilism." She defines it as "an easy-going acceptance of meaninglessness."[10] This seems pretty self-delusional, but even she admits that this leaves only one arbitrator of intellectual and moral right and wrong, and that is raw power.[11] As Gene Veith points out in his book *Postmodern Times*, "The only consistent position for postmodernists is that all talk of morality, *including their own*, only masks the will to power (italics mine)."[12] This is exactly the situation described in the book of Judges: "Everyone did what was right in his own eyes" (21:25). This anarchy creates a clamor for a ruler who will bring

5. Greer, "Strong connection between Hillary and Obama: It's Alinsky."
6. Allen, "From little ACORNs, big scandals grow."
7. Sebastian, "Obama taught 'Destroy middle class'"
8. Alinsky, *Rules for Radicals*.
9. Sperry, "How Obama is bankrolling a nonstop protest."
   Vadum, "Is ACORN violent unrest in Ferguson?"
10. Carr, *Banalization of Nihilism*.
11. By this admission she unwittingly makes the Biblical point of the ongoing Cosmic Battle between the seed of the serpent, who deny God's ultimate power and authority, and the seed of the woman, who acknowledge God's power and authority over all, through their faith in Jesus Christ.
12. Veith, *Postmodern Times*, 197.

stability, which is why totalitarian regimes use crisis and anarchy to prepare society for takeover.

Use of Crisis and Change To Overthrow and Transform

Rahm Emanuel, Chief of Staff for President Obama and currently Chicago mayor, famously said, "You never want a serious crisis go to waste."[13] Crisis is used, even created, to drive political change. Communist Russia has made a science of this. It is matter-of-factly and chillingly explained in interviews and lectures given by former KGB agent Yuri Bezmenov (Tomas Schuman) during the 1980s (still available on YouTube).[14] The overthrow of nations from within consists of four steps: 1. Demoralization, 2. Destabilization, 3. Crisis, and 4. Normalization. Through this process a society is made to be dissatisfied and ashamed of its history and traditions. Its leaders apologize for and mischaracterize its history. Its agitators protest symbols of the nation such as statues, the flag and the national anthem.

Then comes destabilization in riots, protests, and general lawlessness. This leads to crisis, through which the former values are overthrown. The last step is normalization, or the establishment of the new values. During the crisis stage the population looks for a "savior," a human Messiah, just as the Jews in the Old Testament demanded they be given a king: "So all the elders of Israel gathered together and came to Samuel at Ramah. They said to him, 'You are old, and your sons do not walk in your ways; now appoint a king to lead us, such as all the other nations have'" (1 Sam 8:4–5). And although this greatly displeased Samuel, God said, "[I]t is not you they have rejected, but they have rejected me as their king" (1 Sam 8:7b). The prime dangers of this worldview are rejection of God and submission to man and state. It is the latest battle in the age-old cosmic battle between the seed of the serpent (God deniers)

---

13. Rahm Emanuel, Interview published in The Wall Street Journal, November 19, 2008.

14. Two good videos include: Schuman, "Yuri Bezmenov," YouTube. Bezmenov, "Deception Was My Job," YouTube.

and the seed of the woman (those faithful to God). We will return to the dangers and consequences momentarily, but there are still a few points that must be made to describe the postmodern worldview, which works very well to accomplish step two of overthrowing a Christian nation, destabilization.

Postmodernism and Destabilization of Society

Gene Veith, author of *Postmodern Times*, writes, "[P]ostmodern existentialism teaches that meaning is created by a *social group and its language*. According to this view, personal identity and the very contents of one's thoughts are all *social* constructions" (italics mine).[15] A current example of a social construction is gender self-identification; its biological reality is rejected. Naturally, with this postmodern, existentialist view, one would desire a world as described by the famous mathematician, philosopher, atheist, and socialist, Bertrand Russell:

> "I think the subject which will be of most importance politically is mass produced psychology . . . Although this science will be diligently studied, it will be rigidly confined to the governing class. The populace will not be allowed to know how its convictions were generated. When the technique has been perfected, every government that has been in charge of education for a generation will be able to control its subjects securely without the need of armies or policemen . . . Educational propaganda, with government help [and one might today add—"and tools such as Facebook and Google"], could achieve this result in a generation. There are, however, two powerful forces opposed to such a policy; one is religion; the other is nationalism . . . A scientific world cannot be stable unless there is a world government."[16]

---

15. Veith, *Postmodern Times*, 48.
16. Russell, *The Impact of Science on Society*.

By "scientific world," Russell clearly means one in which the behaviors of the masses are controlled by an elite, privileged few, like himself.

Those who have been strongly influenced in their worldview by postmodernism become impervious to facts and reasoning because they see them entirely through the lens of power plays. Veith writes, "For the deconstructionists, all truth claims are suspect and are treated as a cover-up for power plays."[17] He also says, "If reality is socially constructed, then moral guidelines are only masks for oppressive power and individual identity is an illusion."[18] No wonder postmodernists want to stamp out Christianity and its moral guidelines. They see them as nothing more than tools to deceive so that Christians can gain power. This ideology is perfectly suited for the totalitarian's uses because he seeks to gain power by organizing and maintaining a movement. Hannah Arendt says, "Totalitarian movements are possible wherever there are masses who for one reason or another have acquired the appetite for political organization [such as community organizers]. Masses are not held together by a consciousness of common interest [notice how we more and more are being fragmented into minority groups, all with grievances against others] and they lack that specific class articulateness which is expressed in determined, limited and obtainable goals."[19]

Enter The Crisis Phase

Goals end.[20] Movements potentially never do. Chinese communist leader Mao Tse-Tung was famous for his ideology of "continuous revolution." During the Obama administration we heard it in the continual drumbeat for change. Obama's ideological mentor, Saul Alinsky, calls it "The Ideology of Change." This is a very telling name because the change envisioned does not target solutions or tangible

---

17. Veith, *Postmodern Times*, 56.
18. Ibid., 72.
19. Arendt, *Origins of Totalitarianism*, 414.
20. Goals also have measurable outcomes. As we saw in the last chapter, consideration of outcomes is to be avoided in the establishment of tyranny.

outcomes. The target is not anything external to human beings. Human beings are themselves the target—their minds and actions, their worldviews, their ideologies, their hearts, *their souls*! There is to be continual dissatisfaction, continual crisis, continuous victimhood and blame. It is an ideology of change, as well as a change of ideology. The milieu in which it takes place is one where emotion is paramount and there is no time for deliberative consideration and debate of consequences. President Obama repeatedly excused un-Constitutional actions bypassing the intentionally slow, deliberative workings of Congress by saying the country couldn't afford to wait for Congress to act—we must act now.

Hannah Arendt continues, "Within the organizational framework of the movement . . . the fanaticized members can be reached by neither experience nor argument; identification with the movement and total conformism seem to have destroyed the very capacity for experience."[21] As Veith describes it, "The intellect is replaced by the will. Reason is replaced by emotion. Morality is replaced by relativism. Reality itself becomes a social construct."[22] Truth, reality, authenticity, spontaneity, love, purpose, meaning—all must be placed in submission to the tyranny of the godless and enforced by ideology and raw power. "Such is the destiny of all who forget God; so perishes the hope of the godless" (Job 8:13). Veith identifies a second deadly danger and consequence of this ideology: "Those who believe that moral values are nothing more than the imposition of power may be more likely to use power to suppress their opposition."[23] When a significant portion of society accepts this ideology, working out differences peacefully through rational discussion is no longer possible. The only option remaining to resolve differences is the exercise of power through coercion or violence.

---

21. Arendt, *Origins of Totalitarianism*, 410.
22. Veith, *Postmodern Times*, 28–29.
23. Ibid., 51.

The Final Solution: Normalization and the New World Order

Now let us consider the consequences of postmodernism. Veith says, "If there are no absolutes, the society can presumably construct any values that it pleases and is itself subject to none.[24] All such issues are only matters of power. Without moral absolutes, power becomes arbitrary . . . The belief that reality is socially constructed can only be a formula for totalitarianism."[25] But postmodernism can only gain a significant foothold once society becomes dissatisfied with its current beliefs and traditions. This, remember, is the KGB's step one, demoralization. It is the first and longest step. It takes fifteen to twenty years, the amount of time necessary to educate a generation to disbelieve in moral absolutes and give them time to reach positions of influence in government and society. Yuri Bezmenov, a former KGB operative, in the 1980s said that this had been accomplished beyond the KGB's expectations in America. In light of this, Hannah Arendt's warning is one to take note of: "The true role of totalitarian propaganda is not persuasion but organization."[26] And this organization is directed against anyone and anything that threatens the hegemony of the ruling elite.

As real as is the physical danger, the danger this poses to our souls is greater still. The goal of postmodernism and totalitarianism is the rejection of God. It is a laser-focused attack on our souls, our innermost being. It is much more terrifying and evil than a run-of-the-mill political power grab. The following description borrows heavily from Hannah Arendt's masterful and authoritative work, *The Origins of Totalitarianism*:

---

24. This construction of arbitrary values that others will be subjected to is the realization of the philosophy articulated by the highly influential philosopher, Jean-Paul Sarte when he said: "[M]y self is not a stable, entity that lasts through time; rather, it is a creation that I must make and remake from moment to moment. Not only must I create myself, but I must also create my world. I do so by bestowing values on the world . . . Life has no meaning or value except that which I give to it." Palmer, *Looking at Philosophy*, 372–373.

25. Veith, *Postmodern Times*, 159.

26. Arendt, *Origins of Totalitarianism*, 474.

"[A]uthority, no matter in what form, always is meant to restrict or limit freedom, but never to abolish it. Totalitarian domination, however, aims at abolishing freedom, even at eliminating human spontaneity in general . . . [27] Free consent is as much an obstacle to total domination as free opposition. The arbitrary arrest which chooses among innocent people destroys the validity of free consent, just as torture—as distinguished from death—destroys the possibility of opposition."[28] [Think here of elimination of respect for the rule of law and attacks on those who uphold it, such as law enforcement.] "[C]oncentration and extermination camps . . . are the true central institution of totalitarian organizational power.[29][30] The camps are meant not only to exterminate people and degrade human beings, but also serve the ghastly experiment of eliminating, under scientifically controlled conditions, spontaneity itself as an expression of human behavior and of transforming the human personality into a mere thing."[31]

Their success in achieving this is borne out in the astonishing rarity of suicides in the camps. Only one-half of one percent of deaths could be traced to suicides.[32] The camps actually sought

> "to give permanence to the process of dying itself and to enforce a condition in which both death and life are obstructed equally effectively.[33] Even this isn't enough for the totalitarian. The next decisive step in the preparation of living corpses is the murder of the moral person in man. This is done in the main by making martyrdom, for the first time in history, impossible: This is the real mas-

---

27. Arendt, *Origins of Totalitarianism*, 525.

28. Ibid., 581.

29. "Concentration camps" were actually invented not by Hitler, but by Lenin and Trotsky. Pipes, "Lenin's Gulag," 140–146.

30. Arendt, *Origins of Totalitarianism*, 566.

31 Arendt should know. As a German Jew living during World War II, she was forced to flee her homeland. Ibid., 565.

32. Ibid., 586.

33. Arendt, *Origins of Totalitarianism*, 572.

terpiece of the SS. Their greatest accomplishment . . . In order to be successful, a gesture [such as martyrdom] must have social meaning."[34]

Solzhenitsyn's *The Gulag Archipelago* describes the system in Stalin's Russia from the perspective of one who lived in the camps. He describes the many ways that death was made arbitrary so that attempts to die purposefully, say as a martyr, were made almost impossible. And if someone did, no one would ever hear about it. The horrors of totalitarian rule are never far from fallen man, even in the United States of America because they are the natural, unavoidable, eventual consequence of rejecting God. Without God there is only one arbiter of how life is to be lived—raw power. We are clearly seeing many indicators in the United States of the ascendance of rule by raw power as we have turned from God. Society ruled by godless exercise of power must always have victims. The will to power and to "be God" is empty and unsatisfying without its exertion over others.

While flying home from Chile in February 2007, I read a story in their newspaper. A woman had kept her children locked in a completely dark room for seven years.[35] I thought how that must have been. For the first few days, maybe even weeks, they must have pounded on the door, begging their mother to let them out. I can only guess that as she walked away she felt a sadistic satisfaction at their helplessness. Why did she not let them die? She kept coming back. They at least got enough food to live for seven years. Over time the begging and pounding on the door became less and less and finally stopped. What could it possibly have been like in the darkness? Have you tried to keep up a conversation for hours in complete darkness? After it became clear that you were not getting out today, tomorrow, in a week, never, what would you talk about? You have no tomorrow, no friends, no school, no toys or dolls to play with, nothing but darkness. When these children were finally discovered and brought out, they had lost all emo-

---

34. Ibid., 582.

35. Unfortunately, I did not keep the article and cannot now find the original story.

tions. They didn't know how to laugh or even to cry. They had to be retrained. What this mother did to her children is the same thing the concentration camps attempted. Her will to power—even over her own children—was completely unrestrained. It would have been much kinder to kill them, but that, she must have known, would have only been temporary enjoyment of her power. She wanted to prolong it as long as she could. The will to power that results from a godless, nihilistic worldview always needs victims. Without them, those desiring power are left to face their own true powerlessness.

The One, True Hope

These events clearly illustrate the cosmic battle between God and Satan that is still being fought. Making a personal choice between truth and the Deceiver is not an intellectual question. It is a vital, urgent question for today. C.S. Lewis said, "To find their way, atheists must make sense out of a random first cause, denounce as immoral all moral denunciation, express meaningfully all meaninglessness, and find security in hopelessness."[36] Humanity has witnessed the consequences countless times in the past. Isaiah describes it this way: "So justice is driven back, and righteousness stands at a distance; truth has stumbled in the streets, honesty cannot enter. Truth is nowhere to be found, and whoever shuns evil becomes a prey" (Isa 59:14–15).

The Psalmist asks, "When the foundations are being destroyed, what can the righteous do?" (Ps 11:3).

The answer is simple, but not necessarily easy. While the way of postmodernism is a hopeless, meaningless path to destruction, the truth of Jesus Christ is the path to life, even in an evil world: "Even though I walk through the valley of the shadow of death, I will fear no evil, for you are with me; your rod and your staff, they comfort me" (Ps 23:4). The way to truth and life is to put your faith in Jesus Christ, "the Way and the Truth and the Life" (John

---

36. Lewis, *The Inspirational Writings of C.S. Lewis.*

14:6). It is a commitment of our hearts, our spirits, to him. "God is a spirit, and his worshippers must worship in spirit and in truth" (John 4:24). We must cling to the truth which is Jesus Christ and him crucified, which is revealed in his holy Word: "If you hold to my teaching, you are really my disciples. Then you will know the truth, and the truth will set you free" (John 8:32).

Our hope is Christ. To live is Christ. Postmodernism is a deadly lie because it denies Christ. Paul tells the Thessalonians what happens to those who deny Christ: "They perish because they refused to love the truth and so be saved. For this reason God sends them a powerful delusion so that they will believe the lie and so that all will be condemned who have not believed the truth but have delighted in wickedness. But we ought always to thank God for you, brothers loved by the Lord, because from the beginning God chose you to be saved through the sanctifying work of the Spirit and through belief in the truth" (2 Thess 2:10b–13). Jesus commanded his followers to spread the hope of the gospel to all nations. Wearing the belt of truth, carrying the shield of faith and wielding the sword of the Holy Spirit, which is the word of God (Eph 6:14–17), Christ uses even us to roll back the evils of a godless, postmodern culture and bring the people the one, true hope, Christ Jesus (Rom 15:13; Eph 4:4–6).

Discussion Questions

1. What is the basis for morality in postmodernism?
2. Comment on the following statement: Those with the will to absolute power over others are themselves dependent on their victims.
3. What do Christians have to offer a postmodern culture?

8

Peace, Assurance, Boundaries, and Wonder

"To all perfection, I see a limit; but your commands are boundless"

—PS 119:96

"Once when the king of Syria was warring against Israel . . . he sent there horses and chariots and a great army, and they came by night and surrounded the city. When the servant of the man of God rose early in the morning and went out, behold, an army with horses and chariots was all around the city. And the servant said, 'Alas, my master! What shall we do?' He said, 'Do not be afraid, for those who are with us are more than those who are with them.' Then Elisha prayed and said, 'O Lord, please open his eyes that he may see.' So the Lord opened the eyes of the young man, and he saw, and behold, the mountain was full of horses and chariots of fire all around Elisha." (2 Kgs 6:8, 14-17).

PEACE, ASSURANCE, BOUNDARIES, AND WONDER

Senses

Elisha could see God's hosts around him wherever he went. His servant couldn't. We can't. Elisha was able to see a dimension of reality we can only sense in other ways. We are like blind men groping through life.

One night I was walking with a friend across a pasture where we had never been. I was several steps behind him and could just make out his outline in the dark. We were talking as we walked when suddenly he disappeared—just vanished. I came up behind quickly but carefully, to a ledge and stopped. I called out his name several times, but heard no answer. As I listened I heard far, far below me the sound of a river. I couldn't see twenty feet because of the dark, but it must have been hundreds of feet below. About that time I heard my friend call out. He had landed on another ledge and had the wind knocked out of him. He was okay.

We may not all have experiences like this, but we all understand how it feels to walk in the dark, unsure of the next step, not knowing what might slap us in the face or what cliff we might step off of. When walking in the dark, we are usually more cautious than my friend and I were because we know there are so many things around us that we just can't see. How do we know this? We bump into things in the dark. We understand the true, real world around us through the senses that God gave us. To some he shows more of the world through certain senses than others; for instance, a blind person is typically more in tune with sounds, smell, and touch than a sighted person. Some friends of ours have a son who has an impairment in part of his brain, but other parts of his brain are much more sensitive. For example, he has an incredible sense of hearing—almost beyond belief. He will hear sounds that even their pet dogs don't pick up. One day they were walking around their neighborhood far from their house, too far for anyone to hear the phone inside the house. He kept insisting that the phone was ringing. When they returned to the house, he had been right.

Insects can see parts of the light spectrum that we can't like infrared light. Right now radio and TV waves are passing around us and through us. We can't see or hear them because we are made to be receptive to frequencies of voice, not radio. Does that mean that radio waves don't exist? Of course not. A radio doesn't make the information in radio waves any more or less real. It just makes it intelligible to our senses.

God gave us *six* senses so that we might understand the world around us, the real, true world. He gave us these senses and tied them together in our minds so we are able to grasp the truth that we encounter. Let's say we're walking in the dark and can't see anything. We suddenly step into something wet, *feeling* the wetness with our feet. We don't know if it's a mud puddle or an ocean. If we make a big step will we cross it or fall into deep water? And is it water or something else? We bend down to *smell* it. We might *taste* it. We could throw rocks to know how wide it is by *hearing* them land. Using our other senses, even without sight, we build a picture in our mind of what is truly lying before us. We see it in our mind as if it were visible. If we were blindfolded and touched a big tree trunk in the summer, we would see it in our minds with green leaves, sunlight flickering through them. We would not envision it with the red leaves of fall or leafless as in winter. Why? Because our other senses instantly put everything together in an image in our minds—the warmth of the air around us, the smell of the leaves and we see the tree as it truly is.

Our senses can become more or less sensitive to certain things. In the last chapter I mentioned a story in a Chilean newspaper of three children who had been locked in a dark room by their mother for seven years. Their emotions were essentially dead. They had to be trained to cry. If they looked about a room of people at faces of happiness, kindness, love, they would see none of it because, just as we cannot translate the information contained in radio waves into something we understand without a radio, they lost the ability to translate the information in a smile or laugh or a scream of pain into anything they understand.

We live in the middle of a spiritual world, the same that Elisha lived in. What you see, what you hear and feel, are but shadows of what truly surrounds us. I've been referring to our *six* senses.

Peace, Assurance, Boundaries, and Wonder

The sixth is our spiritual sense. It's impaired right now. John Calvin compared the Bible, the Word of God, to spiritual glasses.[1] With God's Word, we see the spiritual world more clearly. We don't see fully or hear fully with this sense yet. We bump into spiritual things that exist all around us right now. We know they are there. We just cannot see them very clearly. If we don't pay attention we may be like my friend, stepping off the ledge and falling to unknown depths, or like the young children in Chile, unable to understand what is right before their eyes. "What no eye has seen, nor ear heard, nor the heart of man imagined, what God has prepared for those who love him—these things God has revealed to us through the Spirit" (1 Cor 2:9). "For God, who said, 'Let light shine out of darkness,' has shone in our hearts to give the light of the knowledge of the glory of God in the face of Jesus Christ" (2 Cor 4:6).

Although we won't fully see the spiritual life until we reach heaven, God reveals these things to us through his word and his Holy Spirit.

Peace and Happiness

We might feel a certain type of peace when we look out and see the colored leaves of autumn. God's peace comes to us through our sixth sense, our spiritual sense. Yes, it can be explained theologically.[23] But peace is not *understood* through the intellect. It may be articulated and its basis explained through our mental capacities, but it becomes real only when it is sensed and felt. We *have* peace when we *feel* at peace. God's peace gives us optimism because, like Elisha's servant, we "see" with our spiritual sense God's presence where others can't.

Ignacio Fernandez wrote a very interesting book that takes a scientific approach to the study of happiness, particularly in

---

1. McNeill, *Calvin: Institutes of the Christian Religion, Vol. 1*, 70.
2. Westminster Divines, *Confession of Faith*, 75–79.
3. Frame, *Systematic Theology*, chapter 44.

organizations.[4] His data disproves the idea that optimists are out of touch with reality and that grim realists have the best grip on it. In fact, optimists are closer to reality because they are better able to see possibilities that others overlook; therefore, it's the optimist that has the best grasp on reality. Christians should be the greatest optimists on the planet! I think those who have matured in their faith generally are. However, we are often criticized for being out of touch with reality and naive. Lenin said religion—and he was directing this at Christianity—was "the opiate of the masses." In other words, it keeps us in a brain-addled "happy place" that is delusional. While his followers have spent most of the last two hundred years trying to foist their "utopia" on the rest of us, exterminating millions in the process, it should be clear by now that the true "opiate" is the leftist utopia associated with Leninism, Marxism, Maoism, humanism and similar ideologies. As we saw in the last chapters, these God-denying ideologies (worldviews) are truly the delusional "opiates" and are supremely unhappy, in spite of the attempts at "cheerful nihilism."[5] Furthermore, they depend on and encourage continuous dissatisfaction, crisis and anxiety rather than peace. These ideologies are merely the latest in a long march of power grabs always under the guise of goodness, justice, and other higher ideals. It is the same power grab that was taken by Eve reaching for the apple with the promise, "You shall be like God " ringing in her ears. What an intoxicating temptation!

Satan was successful in driving a wedge between man and God, causing the Fall of Man. Adam believed he could take matters into his own hands and turn from God. Satan even tried this with Jesus during his wilderness temptations. He showed our Savior all the kingdoms of the world and said, "[A]ll this power will I give thee . . . if thou wilt worship me" (Luke 4:6–7). Think what utopia Jesus could bring if he just turned away from the Father! Of course Jesus recognized this as a lie. It couldn't happen. But even as an idea, division within the Godhead would bring the exact opposite of utopia. However, for those filled with their own

4. Fernandez, *Felicidad Organizacional*.
5. Carr, *Banalization of Nihilism*.

Peace, Assurance, Boundaries, and Wonder

self-importance this is just too great a temptation to resist. Jesus resisted the temptation, but mankind falls for it again and again. Utopia never ever results. It is always the absolute opposite, yet we never seem to learn.

So, who is really in better touch with reality? Who sees the opportunities—the truth of a better, happier existence—that others overlook, or are blind to? Thanks truly to God, we Christians do! Not because of any merit of our own. It is precisely because we have become aware of our own hopelessness and fallenness and our need for Christ that makes us more in touch with reality. "None is righteous, no, not one" (Rom 3:10). Because we know him, we know happiness and peace. We may not know what tomorrow will bring, but we know who holds tomorrow and it will be great!

Blessings of Boundaries and Wonder

Now that sounds a bit Pollyannaish. Is it? Does it mean that everything will go the way I want it to? Not at all!

And why should it? Would it really be satisfying if things did? Yet we try to make things go our way all the time. An acquaintance of mine, like many children of the 1960s, practiced what I call "buddy parenting." It isn't really parenting at all. You let the child explore, make their own decisions, and generally do whatever they want and always get their way. As with all things New Age, practices are described and named with such positive terms who could possibly disagree? But the reality of what was going on was quite different.

"Exploration" can lead to good or bad. You can "explore" paradise or Auschwitz. What is really wanted is a good tour guide with more knowledge than you to provide context, direction and significance. What is needed are parents! Leaving decision-making to a small child, or even an adult in completely new surroundings, can be frightening.[6] It tells the person, "I don't know anything about this either." A child looks up to parents and wants guidance from them. It is comforting to know there is someone that un-

---

6. This is bad practice even in business. See Hersey and Blanchard, *Management of Organizational Behavior*.

derstands these new and different situations and can guide them through. A child finds peace in knowing that parents have greater understanding and can be trusted to guide them until they are able to understand. By telling them "do this" or "don't do that," the parents are serving as God's image bearers until the child begins to think about God himself and can understand, "May the God of hope fill you with all joy and peace as you trust in him, so that you may overflow with hope by the power of the Holy Spirit" (Rom 15:13). As children grow in knowledge of both the physical and spiritual nature of this world, they begin to find peace in the prayer of Paul: "And the peace of God, which transcended all understanding, will guard your hearts and your minds in Christ Jesus" (Phil 4:7). Parents who don't do this teach their children to trust only in themselves, and this is frightening and disheartening to any sane person. It brings anything but peace.

I give these examples of New Age parenting because there is a connection between peace, assurance, boundaries, and wonder. Along with many other names describing our Savior, his name is "Wonderful" (Isa 9:6). Have you ever considered this name of God? We toss around adjectives with little thought. We may merely use "wonderful" interchangeably with "great" or "fantastic," but it has a different meaning. It has been said that wonder is that possession of the mind which enchants the emotions while never surrendering reason.[7] It is like peering through an open door while still standing outside. We are able to participate in some of the experience, but at a distance. We want more! It has also been said that wonder dies with knowledge.[8] When we know something, we feel we have exhausted our interest in it and it's time to move on to something else. This is also true when we only think we know something, even if we don't. And this is part of the danger of New Age parenting, because it engenders a false sense of knowledge; a conceit and un-merited confidence in one's own ability, since it takes place within very artificial conditions of protection (by the

---

7. Zacharias, *Recapture the Wonder*. 20.

8. Of course, wonder can also increase with knowledge. The idea here is the effect on our wonder when knowledge is thought to be *exhaustive* knowledge.

Peace, Assurance, Boundaries, and Wonder

parent) from the consequences of the child's actions. Even mild forms of discipline employed to teach consequences, such as spanking, are absent. This is analogous to long periods of peace, prosperity and freedom in society. They lull us into complacency of not dying to self and dull our spiritual sense. We develop a conceit, a false sense of our own ability and a loss of wonder about things beyond our ability and reach.

I have two dogs, an older dog and a puppy. The puppy lives in a puppy world of wonder. She sees a leaf blown by the wind and pounces on it and plays with it as only a puppy can. The older dog watches as if to say, "What's the matter with you? It's a *leaf!*" But I take them out to our farm, which is a playground for the older dog, but for the puppy everything is new and frightening. One finds peace, assurance, and wonder within certain boundaries that the other would find confining. The broader boundaries are fruitfully explored by the older dog, but they are frightening and overwhelming for the puppy.

Peace and the optimism that comes from it are planted in our hearts and grow under certain conditions, certain boundaries. Just as a plant thrives with the right amount of water at the right times and dies with too much or too little water, or water at the wrong time, we thrive within the boundaries God gives us. And as a plant strives towards the sun—that energy that gives it life—we reach toward the wonder God gives us. It is a peculiar gift that captures our attention and stimulates us to strive toward it. Peace is reached through wonder and boundaries. Is this not also a description of our hope through faith in Christ?

Faith in Christ: The Bond by which We Transcend to the Sacred

The Psalmist says, "To all perfection I see a limit; but your commands are boundless (119:96)." Ravi Zacharias comments on this passage in a wonderful little book called *Recapture the Wonder*: 'To all perfection'—by that he [the Psalmist] means that to every goal or attainment there is a destination point, a finishing line, a moment of consummation. 'But your commands are boundless' means that there is an inexhaustibility to contentment when one lives within the precepts of God's intended purpose for life . . . that is what I like to call . . . boundless wonder."[9] Wonder and peace are connected. How? We strive for physical and sensual things, heaping them up in our lives hoping to find fulfillment in them, but with no connection beyond our physical and sensual wants, they are empty. We find no fulfillment; no peace. Ravi puts it this way: "The only way to transcend the physical and the sensual while retaining their essential features is to bind them to the sacred."[10] The sacred holds wonder; it is that door we can peer through, but not enter. It is that place of the Holy of Holies. It is like that boundary that the New Age child never was told about—"You can't go there. You're not ready." God made us in his image and placed us in paradise. We could walk with him in the cool of the day. He placed us within boundaries where we could be perfectly happy and at peace. And "God commanded man, saying, 'You may surely eat of every tree of the garden, but of the tree of the knowledge of good and evil you shall not eat, for in the day that you eat of it you shall surely die'" (Gen 2:16–17). "Every boundary set by God," Ravi reminds us, "points to something worth protecting."[11] Wonder, and the peace that comes with it, are protected by God's boundaries.

The boundaries that God has placed around us—his law—don't limit us, but rather protect us and provide a space within which we can find joy and peace, and live. Consider a fish which is made to live in water. If you throw it on land, you may have "freed" it from the limitations of the water where it lived, but its "freedom" only brings death. We are children of God, made in his image. He created us as Pascal said, with "a God-shaped vacuum in the heart . . . which cannot be filled by any created thing, but only by God, the Creator made known through Jesus."[12] Being "freed"

9. Zacharias, *Recapture the Wonder*, 36.
10. Ibid., 65.
11. Zacharias, *Recapture the Wonder*, 36.
12. Pascal. "AZQuotes.com," quote 589335.

Peace, Assurance, Boundaries, and Wonder

of God and his Laws, being "freed" of faith in Jesus Christ makes no more sense than "freeing" a fish from water.

Faith in Christ is that bond through which we cross over from the boundaries of our mortal lives to eternal life. His name is Wonderful. He is the door through which today we glimpse the wonder within and tomorrow we enter as the threshold of our home. Where can we possibly find greater peace than our own home? Home is where the heart is. Can it be that the answer is as simple as that? We spill a lot of theological ink explaining how to obtain the assurance of salvation that gives peace in Christ. But it really isn't complicated. Peace is not understood through the intellect. It becomes real only when it is sensed and felt. We *have* peace when we *feel* at peace. Peace is known in the heart. It is *received* into the heart, not worked out in the mind. John said, "But as many as received him, to them he gave power to become the sons of God, even to them that believe on his name" (John 1:12). Jesus has invited us into his eternal home. He says, "I am the door: by me if any man enter in, he shall be saved, and shall go in and out, and find pasture" (John 10:9). Home truly is where the heart is. There is your assurance. There you will know peace. "For where your treasure is, there you heart will be also" (Matt 6:21).

I travel a lot in my work. I see some beautiful places and meet many interesting people, but I always tire of it and can't wait to come home. There is no place on this earth I would rather be. There is no one I would rather be with than my wife and kids. That is where my heart is in human terms during this earthly life. When I was saved, I invited Christ into my home, into my heart, into my family and I joined his family. I was adopted as his child. I am at home with him, at peace with him—and if you have invited him into your heart, you are too. His name is Wonderful; let us rejoice and be glad in it. Let us know peace in it.

Discussion Questions

1. What could we say is our sixth sense? How does it work?
2. How are peace, assurance, boundaries and wonder connected?

9

Suffering

"[I]f pain, suffering and death have no reasonable explanation at all, even though they are universally experienced, then life itself has no meaning."

—RAVI ZACHARIAS[1]

The Reality of Suffering

THE SEVENTEENTH CENTURY POET John Donne experienced some terrible tragedies during his life. His father-in-law became angry with him and not only got him fired, but also ruined his career in law. So he became a priest. During his first year as a priest his wife died, leaving him to support and raise seven children. A few years later, spots formed on his body and he was diagnosed with bubonic plague. His strength was drained and he lay at the point of death for many days. One day while lying in bed he heard a church bell tolling someone's death. He was unsure at first whether or not it was his own death. Reflecting on this, he wrote one of the most

---

1. Zacharias, *Can Man Live Without God?* 185.

famous passages in all of literature, "No man is an island . . . Never send to know for whom the bell tolls; it tolls for thee."[2]

We are not an island. As individuals living in relationship with each other, we are made in God's trinitarian image—three Persons, individual yet at the same time, one Being, one God. God's essence is perfect relationship. We can't fully grasp what perfect relationship is, but our relational life is our reflection of God's image. John Calvin begins his *Institutes of the Christian Religion* by saying, "Without knowledge of self there is no knowledge of God. Nearly all the wisdom we possess, that is to say, true and sound wisdom, consists of two parts: the knowledge of God and of ourselves."[3] The knowledge of one illuminates and deepens the knowledge of the other in an endlessly expanding cycle. Knox Chamblin, the late pastor and professor at Reformed Theological Seminary, includes relationships to others as well as Calvin's "knowledge of self" as necessary for knowledge of God:

> "Each of us is made for three relationships—to oneself, to other people, and to God. These three are distinguishable from one another, but inseparable. Moreover, each of the three is affected by the relationship that exists between God and other people . . . In seeking to maintain and to develop these relationships, we discover that each entails a struggle; and that these are not three struggles but one, each aspect of which can be understood only in relation to the other two. We also discover to our dismay that the threefold struggle persists; that despite our longings we cannot enter into peace and rest. The struggle to end the struggle, in any or all its dimensions, invariably fails."[4]

It is through this endless struggle that we grow in knowledge and more importantly, we grow as human beings in humble awareness that we are children of God. "Iron sharpens iron, and one man sharpens another" (Prov 27:17).

---

2. Yancey, *Where is God When it Hurts?* 71–72. Also see Donne. "Meditation 17."

3. McNeill, *Calvin: Institutes, Vol. 1*, 35.

4. Chamblin, *Paul and the Self*, 11.

SUFFERING

So we are made in God's trinitarian image for relationships to each other and to God, yet we are also fallen creatures living in a fallen world. The Fall took place because of human choice to rebel against God's wishes for us, so before we get too judgmental of God on what we claim is the unfairness of suffering, we should remember that God isn't pleased with the condition of the world either. In fact, it is only by his grace and mercy and the blood of his own Son, Jesus Christ, that our suffering will end. It is only through our faith in him that we will know that land where every tear will be wiped away (Rev 7:17).

The existence of suffering is not an indication that God lacks compassion. It is a statement to us from God telling us that there are some things more awful than the pain of his children. He not only tells us, but he showed us by accepting death on a cross. C.S. Lewis called suffering God's megaphone.[5] It is almost impossible to get our attention when things are going well for us. But after a terrible car wreck, or upon hearing that you have cancer, God has our attention. And what are we most concerned about at those times? It is almost always what will happen to those we love. Will my children be taken care of? What will my husband or wife do? We ache for their pain more than our own. Remember Chamblin's three relationships: to self, to God and to others. These tragic events give us an acute awareness of our growth in reflecting God's image as human beings. We realize that our being—the totally self-centered being we were born as—demanding everything, all our needs from others—has become one whose concerns are much more about others. Through these events and the associated suffering we have become much more selfless. Do you think that's by accident? God is shaping us for a purpose. Paul reminds us in Romans, "And we know that in all things God works for the good of those who love him" (Rom 8:28). God loved us first; he "shows his love for us in that while we were still sinners, Christ died for us" (Rom 5:8). In response to his love, our love of God gives us this love for others that expands our self-love to encompass them. In turn, that love is also reflected back on us, on God, and on others.

---

5. Lewis, *The Problem of Pain*, 93.

In this manner, God is truly working in all things for the good of those who love him.

Value and Purpose in Suffering

We must believe this to be true, even in suffering. But we don't like to think about suffering. It's like the topic of death—we dread the day when it will come, but we know that it *will* come, so we don't want to think about it any sooner than we have to. That's a mistake for several reasons. The most pragmatic is that we can't predict when our turn will come; if we haven't thought about it beforehand, we will be completely unprepared for it when it comes, thus making our suffering all the more terrible. But there are other reasons for spending some time thinking about it. I don't mean dwelling on suffering in a morbid way, but simply considering its significance and meaning for our lives and for humanity.

Why should we care? Ravi Zacharias, in his book *Can Man Live Without God*, explains, "[I]f pain, suffering and death have no reasonable explanation at all, even though they are universally experienced, then life itself has no meaning."[6] I have a real beef with the way suffering is discussed today. It's quite different than at any other time in our history. We who live in an age of pain medications of all kinds, whose life spans are as long as any time since Methuselah, we who live in a time of relative peace and prosperity—it is our generation that defiantly questions God about suffering.

Philip Yancey, in *Where is God When it Hurts?*, noticed a striking division in books about pain and suffering: "The older ones," he says, "[written] by people like Aquinas, Bunyan, Donne, Luther, Calvin and Augustine, ungrudgingly accept pain and suffering as God's useful agents. These authors do not question God's actions. They merely try to 'justify the ways of God to man.'"[7] Let's not forget that these people lived in times of no pain medication and life spans in the range of thirty to forty years. Consider Bunyan's time

---

6. Zacharias, *Can Man Live Without God?* 185.
7. Yancey, *Where Is God When It Hurts?* preface.

in the filthy, rat-infested prisons of his day and Calvin and Luther's persecutions. Suffering was close to these people. It was a part of everyday life, yet they weren't the ones shaking their fists at God for allowing it. However, modern books make a sharp contrast. Yancey says, "Their authors assume that the amount of evil and suffering in the world cannot be matched with the traditional view of a good and loving God. God is thus bumped from a 'friend of the court' position to the box reserved for the defendant. 'How can you possibly justify yourself, God?' these angry moderns seem to say." What Yancey is describing is a belief that we can pass judgment on God. With this sleight of hand we try to make the guilty judge over the innocent. We are guilty of breaking relationship with God and willfully denying him, yet instead of humbly acknowledging our sinfulness before a holy and righteous God, we shake our fists at him. We in our wickedness attempt to place our sin, for which sinless Christ suffered and died to atone for once for all, back on him.

But look what we're missing if we fail to repent of this—by acknowledging our sin and repenting of it, and by faith placing our hope in Christ, we say with Paul, "[T]hat I may know him and the power of his resurrection, and may share his sufferings, becoming like him in his death, that by any means possible I may attain the resurrection from the dead" (Phil 3:10–11). Jesus told us, "Truly, truly, I say to you, you will weep and lament, but the world will rejoice. You will be sorrowful, but your sorrow will turn into joy . . . I have said these things to you, that in me you may have peace. In the world you will have tribulation. But take heart, I have overcome the world" (John 16:20, 33). Instead of chaining ourselves to the suffering and corruption of this world, we see the true hope and promise in suffering, "provided we suffer with him in order that we may also be glorified with him," Paul says, "For I consider "that the sufferings of this present time are not worth comparing with the glory that is to be revealed to us. For the creation waits with eager longing for the revealing of the sons of God. For the creation was subjected to futility, not willingly, but because of him who subjected it, in hope that the creation itself will be set free from its bondage to corruption and obtain the freedom of the glory of the children of God" (Rom

8:17–21). If we realize our true human condition, our hearts and actions will be more humble. In our humility and seeking—in our brokenness—we find God, and find he is sufficient and his power is made perfect in our weakness (2 Cor 12:9).

So if we *could* eliminate all suffering, this would not be a good thing. Because of our human nature, at least some suffering is actually necessary to mold and refine us. James admonishes us to "consider it pure joy, my brothers, whenever you face trials of many kinds, because you know that the testing of your faith develops perseverance. Perseverance must finish its work so that you may be mature and complete, not lacking anything" (1:2–4). The idea of necessary suffering is so foreign to our comfortable, pampered, modern minds, yet it is an inescapable fact of life. Peter explains the purpose and value in suffering: "In this you greatly rejoice, though now for a little while you may have had to suffer grief in all kinds of trials. These have come so that your faith—of greater worth than gold, which perishes even though refined by fire—may be proved genuine and may result in praise, glory and honor when Jesus Christ is revealed" (1 Pet 1:6–7). Peter not only explained the value of suffering, but in his death as a martyr he gave us an example of willing suffering for Christ's sake.

Responses to Suffering

Very often we don't understand the value and purpose in suffering. We may understand it theologically or intellectually, but not in our hearts. When we are in the middle of it, what matters is what is in our hearts. Aleksandr Solzhenitsyn, who saw and endured more suffering than most of us can even imagine, said this: "Gradually it was disclosed to me that the line separating good and evil passes not through states, nor between classes, nor between political parties either—but right through every human heart."[8] What happens to the state of our hearts when we are faced with our own suffering? People who have studied suffering will tell you

---

8. Solzhenitsyn, *Gulag Archipelago*, Vol. 2, 615.

SUFFERING

that our emotions go through a U-shaped curve.[9] When first confronted with tragedy and suffering, our emotions pass through denial, anger, bargaining and plummet to depression at the bottom of the U. Throughout, we wrestle with the question "Why?" The resolution of that question determines when, or if, we climb up the other side of the U. In other words, the resolution to the question in our hearts dictates the outcome for our lives. For Christians and non-believers alike there are two components to the answer: 1. A certain resignation to what has happened, and 2. the Living Hope, not wishful hope, that we build the rest of our lives around. Let's look at these one at a time.

Resignation

People often turn to the book of Job to understand suffering, and with good reason. Job was an upright and righteous man who suffered tragedies beyond what most of us will ever face. When he was struggling at the bottom of the U, he and his wife had different answers. She said, "Curse God and die." He refused to, but instead pleaded before a just and righteous God for an answer. He had a profound faith in God's justice and righteousness, but he doubted that God could apply his righteousness and justice to Job's own situation. Job demanded a hearing before God. He still needed the explanation of how his suffering fit into God's purpose for him. God answered him with a series of questions including, "Where were you when I laid the earth's foundation?" and, "Have you given orders to the morning, or shown the dawn its place?" Only then did Job realize what he was doing: "My ears had heard of you but now my eyes have seen you. Therefore I despise myself and repent in dust and ashes" (Job 42:5–6). Even though we acknowledge God's righteousness and justice at one level—"My ears have heard of you"—we don't realize how we still fail to trust him—"but now my eyes have seen you and I despise myself."

---

9. Kubler-Ross, *On Death and Dying*.

God questioned Job to show how limited Job's understanding was. It is only when we can honestly say like Job, "Surely I spoke of things I did not understand, things too wonderful for me to know," that we begin to show spiritual maturity. How very hard it is for humans to admit our limitations. Ever since the Fall we have tried to place ourselves where only God belongs. Even for a righteous man like Job, it took not only a series of tragedies to acknowledge that he must simply trust God, but it took God himself lecturing him before he could admit there are "things too wonderful for me to know." This is the resignation part of the answer to the question of suffering. Once we acknowledge that there are certain things we will never know and we must trust God on, we are freed to again experience hope. We can confidently place our hope in God's hands and that is our bridge to the answer upon which we build.

Our Living Hope

Although our suffering is still painful, we know that God is good, righteous and just, so there is reason for hope instead of despair. He is our Living Hope. In the mature Christian, there is reason for joy, even during our suffering. Paul said, "[I]n all our troubles my *joy* knows no bounds" (2 Cor 7:4b, italics mine). How can this be? Chesterton argued, "[F]or the Christian, joy is the central feature of life, and sorrow is peripheral because the fundamental questions of life are answered and the peripheral ones are relatively unanswered. For the antitheist, sorrow is central and joy is peripheral because only the peripheral questions are answered and the central ones remain unanswered."[10] I believe this is exactly right. Just pause and consider that we have a holy and righteous God who is in control. He is just, and he loves us so much that he sent his one and only Son to teach us the gospel of his love through his life, death and resurrection. We live in the time of the already and the not yet. Christ has already won the victory over death through his work on the cross of Calvary. We await the consummation of this

10. Zacharias, *Can Man Live Without God?* 186.

victory upon his return. We don't know what tomorrow will bring, but we do know who holds tomorrow and it is in good hands. We share a living and true hope. Non-believers don't. The best they can do is to cling to a false hope of a false god, or a utopian world that they naively feel they can help build. Their tomorrow holds nothing but disappointment and despair.

Ravi Zacharias puts it this way: "How can thinking men and women ever be given ultimate hope when life itself is death-bound? Any hope imparted is only realized by robbing reality in order to pay appearances."[11] But men and women do rob reality to pay appearances all the time. Theologian Peter Kreeft says "Modernity has substituted ideology for truth. An ideology is a man-made system of ideas."[12] The ideology that is most powerfully challenging Christianity today is liberalism in its various God-denying forms, such as socialism, atheism, and Marxism. They all promise a utopian world, if only they are rigorously followed. They promise peace with evil through discussion and appeasement because they deny humanity's evil nature. They detest compromise systems like capitalism and separation of powers in government because these systems acknowledge humanity's imperfection. Their utopias never work in real life. Dostoyevski witnessed these types gain influence in Russia and said this about them: "Love in action is a harsh and dreadful thing compared with love in dreams. For love in action has to choose, while love in dreams can just dream vague, comfortable, all-embracing dreams."[13] Somewhere buried within this statement lies the truth that we seek when we grapple with suffering. Love in dreams is our creation. We own it. We can see all the beautiful happy endings in our dreams. We are the conquering hero riding off into the sunset with the beautiful girl. It's a self-worshipping fantasy that has no room for God, unless it's a bit part. Love in action is messy and unavoidably shows our incompetence, weakness and helplessness. It highlights our utter dependence on God. As Paul learned through his thorn in the flesh, though

---

11. Ibid. 50.
12. Kreeft, *Making Choices*, 127.
13. Dostoyevsky, *The Brothers Karamazov*.

he pleaded with God to take it away, God told him, "My grace is sufficient for you, for my power is made perfect in weakness." Only then was Paul able to say, "Therefore I will boast all the more gladly about my weaknesses, so that Christ's power may rest on me ... For when I am weak, then I am strong" (2 Cor 12:9–10).

A repeating theme in this book is the importance of understanding our human condition and our place before God. If we only acknowledge that we are sinful by nature, deserving of God's wrath and totally dependent on him for our needs and happiness, our lives become infinitely better. I don't mean that we become better in terms of this world's measures. I mean that this world's measures become far less important to us. They may eventually become to us like they were to Paul, "dung" (Phil 3:8). Chesterton says, "Despair does not lie in being weary of suffering, but in being weary of joy."[14] Christ is our wellspring of joy. Peter says, "But rejoice insofar as you share Christ's sufferings, that you may also rejoice and be glad when his glory is revealed" (1 Pet 4:13). Yes, we will suffer in this life, but know that "this light, momentary affliction is preparing for us an eternal weight of glory beyond all comparison, as we look not to the things that are seen but to the things that are unseen. For the things that are seen are transient, but the things that are unseen are eternal" (2 Cor 4:17–18). This isn't in any way to minimize the anguish and pain that we do suffer, but rather to find our purpose and meaning in them. "For it has been granted to you that for the sake of Christ you should not only believe in him but also suffer for his sake" (Phil 3:29); "Now I rejoice in my sufferings for your sake, and in my flesh I am filling up what is lacking in Christ's afflictions for the sake of his body, which is the church" (Col 1:24).

Now there is one final issue I want to deal with, if only briefly, and that is guilt. This is a topic deserving of much more space than we have. We may understand suffering with our minds, but when we experience it with our hearts, we often see our suffering as God's judgment upon us for our sins. Don't do this! Don't say things like, "Because I had an abortion twenty years ago my little

---

14. Zacharias, *The Real Face of Atheism*, 84.

girl has been struck down with disease today." This is poison and it denies Christ's atoning work that washed away our sins. We could all give examples in which a person's suffering seems out of proportion to their sins, especially when it comes to young children. Don't act like Job and try to outguess God. As believers we are part of one body, the body of Christ. We belong not just to ourselves, but to each other and to Christ. When one of us suffers we are all affected; though we may never see the connection, it is there nevertheless. Be satisfied knowing that we have a loving and righteous God. He suffered for us and continues to love us in our suffering. He is our hope today, tomorrow, and throughout eternity.

Discussion Questions

1. We are made in God's trinitarian image and live in a fallen world. What is the practical implication of this for our lives?

2. Does the existence of suffering mean God lacks compassion?

Heidelberg Catechism

Lord's Day 1: What is your only comfort in life and in death?

That I am not my own, but belong—body and soul, in life and in death—to my faithful Savior Jesus Christ. He has fully paid for all my sins with his precious blood, and has set me free from the tyranny of the devil. He also watches over me in such a way that not a hair can fall from my head without the will of my Father in heaven: In fact, all things must work together for my salvation. Because I belong to him, Christ, by his Holy Spirit, assures me of eternal life and makes me whole-heartedly willing and ready from now on to live for him.

Lord's Day 2: What must you know to live and die in the joy of this comfort?

Three things: first, how great my sin and misery are; second how I am set free from all my sins and misery; third, how I am to thank God for such deliverance.

10

Giving Thanks In All Things

"[G]ive thanks in all circumstances; for this is the will of God in Christ Jesus for you."

—1 THESS 5:18

Giving Thanks In All Things

I'VE LONG BEEN IN the habit of beginning my prayers with thanks. After all, there is so much that God has blessed me with. His Holy Spirit has filled my home with love, in spite of what I sometimes do to disrupt it. I have been blessed with good health, in spite of how I eat. My wife and kids have been healthy and my wife's cancer has not recurred. I am able to provide for my family's needs, although I have known times when I couldn't. I live in a place that I've always wanted to live. I could fill books reciting examples of God's blessings in the face of my shortcomings. We have a loving God, who delights in our happiness.

You may have noticed that my list of blessings was pretty self-centered. It was basically about what I wanted for me and my family. It is easy to give thanks when we get what we want. Even the most immature Christian can do this because early in our walk with Jesus it's still all about us. Pretty quickly, that sphere widens to include others; at least, we begin to recognize the need for looking beyond ourselves to the needs of others. You may remember from the last chapter, I quoted Knox Chamblin who made the point that there are three relationships that help us display God's image: the relationship to oneself, to other people, and to God. Because we live in a fallen world, these relationships are not in perfect harmony and entail a life-long struggle. However, by trusting in God throughout our struggle we grow towards more perfect relationships, which more perfectly reflect God's image on earth.[1]

As we grow in our faith and study God's Word and his trinitarian Being, we begin to understand that we are made to serve others and God. In so doing we find fulfillment, meaning, and happiness. As we journey along this part of our walk with God, we find more challenges. We stretch beyond our self-centeredness to that next realm of comfort—our friends and loved ones. It isn't always easy, but we slowly begin to give thanks for things we would never have imagined being thankful for earlier in our lives. We may resist his call to serve him, like Jonah did (Jonah 1:1–3). We may try to hide from the task he has for us, rather than thanking him for choosing us—like Elijah did (1 Kgs 19:1–9). But he does know best. He is shaping us while he stretches us. He is preparing us to fulfill our potential, but our conception of our potential is far too limited. We conceive our potential by human measures such as career, money, or social status. These things pass and are quickly forgotten. God is preparing us to fulfill a potential that we can't begin to fully grasp—reflecting his glorious image throughout eternity and knowing the perfection of love with our brothers and sisters in Christ. So he stretches us beyond our self-centered desires for our well-being to learn to desire and give thanks for the well-being of others.

We can understand this. We may hem and haw and grumble and resist, but in the end we can see the value in this attitude, and any moderately-serious believer, as well as very many non-believers, strive to give sincere thanks for the well-being of others.

---

1. Chamblin, *Paul and the Self*, 11

Giving Thanks In All Things

But then as we continue to study God's Word, we run into this: "Be joyful always; pray continually; give thanks in all circumstances, for this is God's will for you in Christ Jesus" (1 Thess 5:18). What do you make of that? Surely we can't take that to literally mean we should give thanks in *all* circumstances, right? Well, what about Psalms 34:1, "I will extol the Lord at all times; his praise will always be on my lips"? Or maybe Ephesians 5:19–20, "Speak to one another with psalms, hymns and spiritual songs. Sing and make music in your heart to the Lord, always giving thanks to God the Father for everything, in the name of our Lord Jesus Christ." Or Philippians 4:6, "Do not be anxious about anything, but in everything, by prayer and petition, with thanksgiving, present your requests to God." Still another, "And whatever you do, whether in word or deed, do it all in the name of the Lord Jesus, giving thanks to God the Father through him" (Col 3:17). And if we still doubt it, "Through Jesus, therefore, let us continually offer to God a sacrifice of praise—the fruit of lips that confess his name" (Heb 13:15).

So there is really no getting around this appeal to give thanks in all circumstances. But let's not lose sight of what we are being told. We are not told to give thanks to the drunk driver who kills a son or daughter. We are not being told to give thanks to the man who sues us frivolously to take our money. We are told to give thanks *to God* in all things. And neither are we to be thankful that we, or others, have pain or suffering, but we are to be thankful that God is there for us in our pain and suffering and that in all things God works for the good of those who love him (Rom 8:28).

Are there examples where people have actually lived this in their lives? Absolutely! Let me give a few examples from Scripture.

Unexpected Blessings

In Acts we are told of when Paul and Silas were thrown in prison (16:16–34). In Rome, when you were sent to prison they didn't take your fingerprints and make you fill out a lot of forms. You were stripped and beaten severely. You had no clothes to absorb any of the violence. You were sent to your cell bloody and bruised—eyes swollen, cuts stinging, and everywhere aching and tender. Then Paul and Silas were locked in an inner cell in stocks. Being placed in stocks was a form of torture because your feet were placed apart at an uncomfortable distance and you couldn't move them. After their beating, Paul and Silas could hardly stand anyway, much less for hours on end with their feet locked into place and no support for their upper body. It was in this condition during the middle of the night that they began praying and singing hymns to God. In this particular case, God saved them from this situation through an earthquake. As a result, Paul saved the jailer from committing suicide and through Paul and these events, God brought the jailer and his family to saving faith. Though they couldn't have imagined how things would play out, Paul and Silas gave thanks to God even while suffering from the stocks and their wounds. From a human perspective they had nothing to be thankful for and could look to a morning that would likely be worse still. But they had transcended their human situation through faith in Christ.

And what of the story of Joseph? He was sold into slavery by his own brothers. His father was told that he was dead. Joseph worked his way into a very influential position and was brought down and thrown into prison by the false accusation of his master's wife. The story goes on with Joseph again gaining an influential position, second only to the Pharaoh. Eventually he wound up saving not only his father, but also the very brothers that sold him into slavery. He told them, "You intended to harm me, but God intended it for good to accomplish what is now being done, the saving of many lives" (Gen 50:20). Throughout his many years of personal tragedies and hard struggles to recover from them, he was not bitter. He knew God was using him for a purpose.

Then there is the story of Daniel. Nebuchadnezzar, king of Babylon, brought Daniel from conquered Judah as a servant, but he rose to become one of the king's best wise men. God used him in many unforeseen ways by placing Daniel where he did.

The Bible is full of examples of people who faced terrible difficulties in their lives, yet continued to give thanks to God. And God remembered them, and *remembers* us today.

Giving Thanks In All Things

What about in more recent times? Are there still people who give thanks in all things, even during their darkest moments? Of course there are. I only have space for one example.

I quote liberally from a dialogue. The entire book is well worth reading. It is *The Hiding Place,* and tells the real-life experience of Corrie Ten Boom.[2] It's an amazing story about her family in Holland, who were hiding Jews in their home during World War II. They were eventually discovered and Corrie, her father, and her sister Betsie were sent to concentration camps. They endured a horrific ordeal in which her father and sister eventually died, and Corrie was only released due to a clerical error one week prior to her group being gassed to death.

In the course of the story, Betsie and Corrie had been moved about to various prisons and camps, but had managed to stay together. Now they arrived in the dreaded Ravensbruk camp. Few ever left it. After passing through the usual humiliating stripping, they were herded into a dark, crowded room filled with straw-covered platforms where they would live and sleep. Corrie begins, "We lay back, struggling against the nausea that swept over us from the reeking straw . . . Suddenly I sat up, striking my head on the cross-slats above. Something had pinched my leg. 'Fleas!' I cried. 'Betsie, the place is swarming with them! . . . [H]ow can we live in such a place!'" Bestie answered by pointing Corrie back to Scripture from First Thessalonians they had been able to clandestinely read a few hours earlier.

> "[P]ray constantly, give thanks in all circumstances; for this is the will of God in Christ Jesus—'That's it, Corrie!,' Betsie replied, 'That's his answer. Give thanks in all circumstances! That's what we can do. We can start right now to thank God for every single thing about this new barracks!' I stared at her, then around me at the dark, foul-aired room. 'Such as?' I said. 'Such as what you're holding in your hands.' I looked down at the Bible. 'Yes! Thank You, Dear Lord, that there was no inspection when we entered here! Thank You for all the women,

---

2. Ten Boom, Sherrill and Sherrill, *The Hiding Place,* 188–209.

here in this room, who will meet You in these pages.' 'Yes,' said Betsie. 'Thank You for the very crowding here. Since we're packed so close, that many more will hear!' She looked at me expectantly. 'Corrie!' she prodded. 'Oh, all right. Thank You for the jammed, crammed, stuffed, packed, suffocating crowds.' 'Thank You,' Betsie said serenely, 'for the fleas and for —' The fleas! This was too much. 'Betsie, there's no way even God can make me grateful for a flea.' 'Give thanks in all circumstances,' she quoted. 'It doesn't say, in pleasant circumstances. Fleas are part of this place where God has put us.' And so we stood between piers of bunks and gave thanks for fleas. But this time I was sure Betsie was wrong."[3]

And so the story continues for several pages. Their work was brutally hard all day, but when they returned to their flea-ridden barracks at night there was intense interest in Bible study with the one little Bible they had been able to smuggle in. Betsie's health took a turn for the worse. She was given a few days off work, but no medical treatment. Even this little rest was beneficial. So when she returned to work, still fevered, Corrie noticed some improvement.

"Betsie was waiting for me, as always, so that we could wait through the food line together. Her eyes were twinkling. 'You're looking extraordinarily pleased with yourself,' I told her. 'You know we've never understood why we had so much freedom in the big room,' she said. 'Well—I've found out.' That afternoon, she said, there'd been confusion in her knitting group about sock sizes and they'd asked the supervisor to come and settle it. 'But she wouldn't. She wouldn't step through the door and neither would the guards. And you know why?' Betsie couldn't keep the triumph from her voice: 'Because of the fleas! That's what she said, 'That place is crawling with fleas!'"[4]

Even in those things where we see no possible reason for giving thanks, God is still at work. Whether in this life or the

---

3. Ibid.
4. Ibid.

next we know, "[A]ll things work together for good to them that love God" (Rom 8:28).

You may be thinking those are nice examples of how things worked out well for people who continued to give thanks to God even in circumstances in which a happy ending was almost impossible to expect. But what about those who never see a happy ending? We Christians are frequently confronted with just this question. And the answer really isn't complicated. One must first and foremost consider the basis these people had for giving thanks in terrible and seemingly hopeless situations. The basis was their relationship with God and their firm trust in his promises. They couldn't see to what greater purpose they were contributing. But they knew it existed. Think of the story of Joseph, whose brothers sold him into slavery. God used him to eventually save them and many others from starvation. He told them, "[Y]ou meant evil against me, but God meant it for good" (Gen 50:20). The people in the examples above had an unshakeable confidence in life beyond this earthly life. Therefore, their current troubles—terrible though they might be—were temporary. They were more concerned with serving God and obeying to him than they were the consequences or trials they might face in this life. For example, Shadrach, Meshach and Abednego refused to disobey God's command against worshipping idols, even when faced with what seemed to be certain death from disobeying King Nebuchadnezzar's command to worship an idol. He told them that they would be thrown into a furnace if they didn't obey him, and taunted them saying, "And who is the god who will deliver you out of my hands?" (Dan 3:15). But they answered him not knowing God's decision for their fate on this matter, but perfectly at peace in the knowledge of God's omnipotence and eternal promise for them. So they replied, "O Nebuchadnezzar, we have no need to answer you in this matter. If this be so, our God whom we serve is able to deliver us from the burning fiery furnace, and he will deliver us out of your hand, O king. But if not, be it known to you, O king, that we will not serve your gods or worship the golden image that you have set up" (Dan

3:16–18). There have been countless other examples of Christian faithful responding in the same way.[5]

The basis upon which we can give thanks in all things is faith in God and, since Jesus's coming in the flesh, faith in Jesus Christ. "Now faith is the assurance of things hoped for, the conviction of things not seen" (Heb 11:1). This chapter of the book of Hebrews continues listing several examples of people who acted in faith to God's commands and promises, and, "These all died in faith, not having received the things promised, but having seen them and greeted them from afar, and having acknowledged that they were strangers and exiles on the earth . . . they desire a better country, that is a heavenly one" (Heb 11:13–16). They were thankful to God in this life, knowing that this life is temporary and not their home. Though not giving thanks for their trials and suffering, these faithful people of God gave thanks to him even during their trials because of what lay ahead. They "suffered mocking and flogging, and even chains and imprisonment. They were stoned, they were sawn in two, they were killed with the sword. They went about in skins of sheep and goats, destitute, afflicted, mistreated—of whom the world was not worthy—wandering about in deserts and mountains, and in dens and caves of the earth. And all these, though commended through their faith, did not receive what was promised, since God had provided something better" (Heb 11:36–40a).

Our Thanks and Our Lord's Example

We can't complete our discussion of this topic without considering the greatest example of giving thanks in all things: "The Lord Jesus, on the night he was betrayed, took bread, and when he had given thanks, he broke it and said, 'This is my body, which is for you; do this in remembrance of me'" (1 Cor 11:23b–24). Jesus was awaiting his death. This was the very night he was to be betrayed, and by one he was sharing his food with! What man, even Jesus, could face that moment with anything but a heavy heart? The time of his

---

5. Examples abound throughout history. A classic book collecting a number of examples is by John Foxe. *Foxe's Book of Martyrs*.

death would be soon and it would not be quick, but agonizing and humiliating. His flesh and muscle would be ripped off down to the bone. His hands and feet would be nailed, *nailed* to a cross. There he would hang, unable to even scratch the few uncut places on his body as his trickling blood tickled his skin, and unable to chase away the flies that began to light on his hands and face. This lay just hours before him, thanks to the man who had been his friend, whose hand was now with his in the bowl of food. Could you give *thanks* at that moment? Jesus didn't thank Judas for what he would do. He said, "[W]oe to that man who betrays the Son of Man. It would be better for him if he had not been born" (Mark 14:21), and, "What you are about to do, do quickly" (John 13:27). But he gave thanks to the Father not just for the meal, but more importantly, for the purpose which he was fulfilling as the Son. This strengthened him to look past the ordeal that lay immediately ahead to the glorious purpose; he broke the bread saying, "This is my body, *which is for you*!" And in the same way he took the cup saying, "This cup is the new covenant in my blood; do this . . . in remembrance of me. For whenever you eat this bread and drink this cup, you *proclaim the Lord's death* until he comes" (1 Cor 11:25-26, italics added). This is where a non-believer becomes baffled. What purpose does it serve to proclaim your Lord's *death*? And this is where we as believers find hope and the voice to lift up thanks to God from the depths of our darkest hours. We proclaim his death because, "While we were yet sinners, Christ died for us" (Rom 5:8), and because, "[A]ll of us who were baptized into Christ Jesus were baptized into his death. We were therefore buried with him through baptism into death in order that, just as Christ was raised from the dead through the glory of the Father, we too may live a new life. If we have been united with him like this in his death, we will certainly also be united with him in his resurrection" (Rom 6:3–6). By faith in Christ's substitutionary work on the cross of Calvary we Christians know peace in this life and the hope of an eternal life in heaven beyond this one. We know a better, permanent home awaits us. Because of Christ's life, death and resurrection, fulfilling God's eternal plan of salvation, we give thanks in all things!

Discussion Questions

1. Discuss the promise in the Biblical passage that explains why we should give thanks to God in *all* things? (Rom 8:28, "And we know that all things work together for good to them that love God, to them who are the called according to his purpose.")

2. Can you give an example in your life that you give God thanks for that would seem strange in human terms?

11

Crossroads of the Eternal

"Just as we have borne the image of the man of dust, we shall also bear the image of the man of heaven"

—1 COR 15:49

Human, Spirit and Our True Being

THE FRENCH PHILOSOPHER PIERRE Teilhard de Chardin said, "We are not human beings having a spiritual experience. We are spiritual beings having a human experience."[1] This isn't the best theology, but I liked it because it mentioned something that we are very confused about today—the spiritual world. So far, we've discussed ideologies and worldviews that deny God and the spiritual world, such as postmodernism and atheism. There also are many people who are just fine with "spirituality" as long as it isn't Christian spirituality, because they practice a "spirituality" which only they can define. Part of what I like about de Chardin's quote is that it disputes the validity of our spiritual nature being something we define and control:—"We are not human beings having a spiritual *experience*" (italics mine); that is to say, our spiritual experience

---

1. de Chardin, "AZQuotes.com," quote 53365.

is not within our ability to control and manipulate as we would, say an experience at the beach. Rather, *it* defines *us*. However, our ability to manipulate our spiritual experience is a typical attitude of "spiritual" people, as opposed to Christians.

De Chardin also denies postmodern and atheistic claims by saying, "We are spiritual beings having a human experience"; we are spiritual, not strictly materialistic beings. But he errs in staking his claims in the dangerous territory of dualism. Our true identity is not *either* human *or* spiritual. It's both. "The essence of a human being," according to Reformed theologian Herman Bavinck, "consists above all in the most intimate union of soul and body in a single personality."[2]

We have no trouble recognizing our physical, human nature—we glorify it and idolize it, as is evident in the behavior that is rewarded in our pop culture. But modern man has a much more difficult time acknowledging the spiritual nature of his being. Those who do are often uncomfortable admitting their place in relation to God. In chapter 1 we discussed God's revelation to us, how one worldview believes everything, including God, resides within the "box" of natural law, while the Christian worldview recognizes that God is not contained in the box of nature, but exists outside of it. Then in chapter 2 we studied the assumptions upon which we base our knowledge of truth and saw afresh how the fear of God and faith in Christ are the only ways to true knowledge of anything that really matters. In a sense, we reasserted the validity of that neglected part of our person, our spiritual side. Or, better said, our *spirit* since it isn't a "side," as if part of a schizophrenic personality, but it is as much a part of us as our eyes and ears. Our physical body parts equip us for life in the physical realm; our spirit does likewise in the spiritual realm. Paul explains it this way:

> "'What no eye has seen, nor ear heard, nor the heart of man imagined, what God has prepared for those who love him—these things God has revealed to us through the Spirit . . . Now we have received not the spirit of the world, but the Spirit who is from God, that we might

2. Bavinck, *Reformed Dogmatics*, Vol. 4, 694.

understand the things freely given us by God. And we impart this in words not taught by human wisdom but taught by the Spirit, interpreting spiritual truths to those who are spiritual. The natural person does not accept the things of the Spirit of God, for they are folly to him, and he is not able to understand them because they are spiritually discerned" (1 Cor 2:9–14).

Just as God gave us physical eyes to see the physical world, he reveals the spiritual world to us through his Holy Spirit. God made us perfectly adapted for our world, and our world is a physical *and* spiritual one. As a biologist, I never tire of learning the minute details with which God made animals and plants particularly well-suited for their environments. He gave penguins a metabolism and body that keep them warm in icy waters when temperatures drop far below zero. They have special characteristics that allow them to lay eggs and warm and hatch them on ice or frozen ground. He made the Gila monster able to live in the desert and not drink water for weeks, or even months. He made his creation exquisitely well-suited for the world he placed them in, and we are no different. When we deny God and our spiritual nature we are like a penguin attempting to live in the hot desert, or a Gila monster attempting to swim in arctic waters. We attempt to live only in a physical world, yet that isn't our world. Our world is one in which physical and spiritual realms are intimately intertwined. Think of the real but hidden world that was revealed to Elisha's servant, full of horses and chariots of fire (2 Kgs 6:14–17). Our world is a union of physical and spiritual realms, and our essence as humans consists of a most intimate union of body and spirit in a single personality. That essence remains after the Fall. What was lost at the Fall was our union with Christ.

Bound to the Timeless

We are made in God's trinitarian image and our character and being reflect the Trinity in many ways that the great theologian John

Frame, calls "triperspectivalism."[3] It's a fancy term for recognizing the Trinity reflected all around and within us in God's design of his creation. A triperspectival view of human beings would add to Bavinck's description the fact that we are not only an intimate union of soul and body in a single personality; we as Christians are a union of soul, body and Christ. The life of our soul and body is animated in Christ by the Holy Spirit. Turning from Christ is death—body and soul. Bavinck explains it this way:

> "By virtue of their creation, humans are linked with nature and the human world, visible and invisible things, heaven and earth, God and angels. And they live if, and to the degree that, they stand in the right, that is, in the God-willed relation to the whole of their surroundings. Accordingly, in its essence and entire scope, death is disturbance, the breakup of all these relations in which humans stood originally and still ought to stand now. Death's cause, therefore, is and can be none other than the sin that disturbs the right relation to God and breaks up life-embracing fellowship with God. In this sense sin not only results in death but also coincides with it; sin is death, death in a spiritual sense. Those who sin, by that token and at the same moment, put themselves in an adversarial relationship toward God, are dead to God and the things of God, have no pleasure in the knowledge of his ways, and in hostility and hatred turn away from him."[4]

Ezekiel simply says, "The soul who sins shall die" (Ezek 18:20).

When Adam ate the forbidden fruit at Eve's prompting believing the serpent's promise that they would become like God fellowship with God was lost and sin and death entered the world. In his commentary on Genesis, Victor Hamilton says, "Alas, rather than experiencing bliss, they encounter misery. Rather than sitting on a throne, they are expelled from the garden. Rather than new prerogatives, they experience only a reversal. The couple not only

---

3. Frame, *Systematic Theology*, 46.
4. Bavinck, *Reformed Dogmatics, Vol. 4*, 614.

fails to gain something they do not presently have; the irony is that they lose what they currently possess: unsullied fellowship with God. They found nothing and lost everything."[5]

Our three-fold being of body, soul, and Christ, or physical, spiritual, and Christ, was blown apart at the Fall. Like Humpty Dumpty, we've been trying to put ourselves together again ever since. Some attempt to pick up the *spiritual* pieces apart from Christ, only to find a delusion in any of the myriad choices including Islam, Buddhism, Mormonism, paganism, and even things like Marxism, humanism and radical environmentalism. Some try to put the *physical* pieces together by pursuing material success. They may become billionaires or celebrities idolized for their money or physical looks, or more typically, they only wish to be. But without Christ their soul remains shattered, far from Christ. In their pursuit of physical things alone, they remain anxious about their lives. To them Jesus says, "[D]o not be anxious about your life . . . Consider the lilies of the field, how they grow: they neither toil nor spin, yet I tell you, even Solomon in all his glory was not arrayed like one of these . . . Seek ye first the kingdom of God and his righteousness" (Matt 6:25, 28, 33). This is the only way to be restored to that lost state that we long for, free from brokenness—seek ye first the kingdom of God and his righteousness. And Jesus is the only way into that kingdom (John 14:6). By binding ourselves to Christ through faith in his promises, we find our way back from a misguided false dualism to a soul and body unified in Christ, united in his glorious purpose for his creation. In one sense, we are tools in his hand to accomplish his vast purpose for the universe, but in another sense, the universe is his tool for accomplishing his purpose in each of us. That is why Paul can say, "And we know that for those who love God all things work together for good, for those who are called according to his purpose" (Rom 8:28).

In chapter 8 we learned that the way to transcend the physical and the sensual components of life while retaining their essential features is to bind them to the sacred. The Old Testament is filled with pages and pages of detailed descriptions of how to kill,

---

5. Hamilton, *The Book of Genesis: Chapters 1–17*, 208.

dress and burn livestock. Why? Through these ceremonies, God is teaching us how to transcend our physical and sensual existence and reenter the fullness of life that was lost at the Fall—not that we can fully achieve that renewal in this life, but that we might have glimpses, reminders, foretastes of it. He whets our appetite for the great wedding feast (Matt 22:2-14; Rev 19:7-9). He is preparing us for that day when the Lamb returns for his bride the Church.

What are the sacraments if not a means to transcend the physical and sensual by binding them to the sacred? "[T]he Lord Jesus on the night he was betrayed took bread [physical, real bread that we can see, touch, taste, and feel with our senses], and when he had given thanks, he broke it, and said, 'This is my body which is for you. Do this in remembrance of me'" (1 Cor 11:23-24). Through this remembrance, the physical bread that we know with our senses is bound to the sacred and holy, our Lord and Savior Jesus, and the wine likewise. In this remembrance Jesus is asking us also to transcend a merely physical experience to remember our destinies as whole persons—physical and spiritual united as one being in the body of Christ until that time in which our destinies are realized at Christ's return (1 Cor 11:25-26). Similarly, Augustine distinguished between two components of a sacrament—one can be seen, the other is understood; one is physical, the other spiritual. The visible and invisible churches provide another example of the unity of the physical and spiritual realms. The invisible church, i.e.,—those within the visible church who have entered into true spiritual union with Christ,[6] indicates a spiritual aspect of the church and its members are known only to God. The visible church is, of course, the physical. Our world and our very being consist of both the physical and the spiritual. The admonition in Hebrews, "Do not neglect to show hospitality to strangers [physical], for thereby some have entertained angels [spiritual] unawares" (13:2), speaks to the fact that both physical and spiritual beings are living in this world right now.

In chapter 1 we began by looking at God's revelation of himself to us through his creation and through his special revelation (again, the physical and spiritual). We then looked at how we really

---

6. Berkhoff, *Systematic Theology*, 566.

know anything, and it all comes back to knowing him (chapter 2). We saw how we must yield to his authority and be obedient to him for our own happiness and fulfillment (chapters 3 and 4). These are all ways in which we transcend our physical and sensual existence by binding ourselves to the sacred. Most people understand at some level the necessity of transcending our physical and sensual experience by binding it to the sacred. My pagan friends and relatives agree that there is a higher power, and they seek connection with it through nature and "spirituality." Many would agree with G.K. Chesterton's statement, "Take away the supernatural, and what remains is the unnatural."[7] God is stirring their souls, but they are deceived by the world. That is why we spent so much time on truth (chapters 5 through 7). I referred to John 14:6 in almost every chapter: Jesus said, "I am the Way and the Truth and the Life. No one comes to the Father except through me." There is no getting around that. And there really is no truth apart from God. Reformed Theological Seminary theologian John Frame says, "If God is in control of the world, the world is under his control. If God is our supreme authority, then he has the right to tell us what to believe. And if he is present everywhere, our attempts to know the world ought to recognize that presence. The most important fact about anything in the world is its relationship to God's lordship."[8]

The most important fact about our own lives is our relationship to God and his lordship—the very relationship we turned away from at the Fall. Can you think back to that first relationship— maybe your first sweetheart—that seemed so perfect? Everything in your life revolved around her (or him) and you wanted it to last forever. It was a glimpse of that blissful, perfect relationship that exists in the Godhead, but by our sin we are not worthy to know any more. It is only by God's grace that we experience those glimpses. For over thirty years with my sweetheart I've had the joy of many glimpses of what that perfect relationship will be. But of course they are only glimpses, and our love is sustained through our difficult periods by those glimpses. It is just these glimpses of the immortal

---

7. Chesterton, *Heretics*, 50.
8. Frame, *Systematic Theology*, 701.

that Chesterton was thinking about when he said, "Man cannot love mortal things. He can only love immortal things for an instant."[9] And so we treasure those instants, those glimpses of the eternal love that we will know in heaven, when we will shed our perishable and corrupt bodies and rise imperishable, when our sinful hearts are made whole, where there will be no more tears (Rev 7:17).

Life At the Crossroads of the Eternal

Back when I was pastoring a church in Iowa, we started an annual homecoming at a small historic chapel that the early settlers had built. It sat on a low hill surrounded by cornfields. It had no electricity. There still were some old wood heaters that had been used during the frigid Iowa winters scattered amongst the pews. Our service was always held during Memorial Day weekend. We opened the big window shutters and let the breeze pass through during the service. We also left the front door open and I looked out from the pulpit upon a corral of cattle, which we could hear lowing during pauses in our prayers. I think our first service was in 2006, but, except for the cars out front and the recording equipment inside, it could have been 1906, 1806 or 1706. People came from all over the country for this homecoming. We even had some from overseas. Why? What did people see at this primitive little chapel in the Iowa plains surrounded by corn and cattle?

People today live at a very unique time in the history of mankind. I can wake up in Rome, Italy and by evening be comfortably in my home in North Carolina. The world and all its splendor is open for us to experience, from the peaks of the Alps to the Great Barrier Reef of Australia; from Michelangelo's Sistine Chapel to the pyramids of Egypt to the lost city of Machu Picchu, the greatest works of mankind are there for us to experience. Many people spend their lives doing just that, and these things can be great blessings to us. But there is a greater longing that people seek in these experiences. We each have it deep down in our very

---

9. Chesterton, *Heretics*, 56.

souls, but we can't put our finger on it. From high up along the Blue Ridge Parkway near my home, we might look out across the ancient Appalachian mountains to watch the sun slowly disappear behind them and something very powerful touches our emotions.

Why should we feel this way? It makes no sense. It's nothing new. It is a scene that our fathers and grandfathers might have seen. It is the same sun going down behind the same mountains that the Cherokee watched. Indeed, it is a scene that was majestically playing out even long before the first Cherokee sat hand-in-hand to watch it with his young maiden. Like many of these experiences, it is so predictable, so common, so timeless. And my friends, here is the answer: it is the timeless we long for. We are made for the timeless, the eternal. Our souls know this even when our minds do not. Our souls are drawn by these scenes to transcend our physical lives and bind them to the eternal. We are like prisoners looking from the prison cells of this mortal life at the home we have been banished from by the guilt of our sins. The cherubim bar the door and prevent our return. In these moments we catch a fleeting glimpse of the home we long for. How do we break free from our cells, reach beyond them and reconnect with the timeless, the eternal? Jesus said, "Truly, truly, I say unto you . . . I am the door. If anyone enters by me, he will be saved and will go in and out" (John 10:7–9). He is the Good Shepherd. "The sheep hear his voice, and he calls his own sheep by name and leads them out. When he has brought out all his own, he goes before them, and the sheep follow him, for they know his voice" (John 10:1–4).

Whether they knew it or not, this longing is what drew people from all over to that little chapel. Sitting in that primitive chapel on the lonely plains of Iowa, grandmothers sat beside their sons, daughters, and grandchildren in the same pews where they had sat as children. They bowed their gray heads before their Lord and Savior just as their parents and grandparents before them. Grandchildren looked up at the muscular old hands of their grandfather, weathered by a life of farming the Iowa cornfields, clasped together in humble and earnest prayer for forgiveness of things neglected and now with too little time left to do them. Oh, but could their grandchildren only avoid repeating their mistakes! But they won't. They haven't yet realized the confines of their prison cells. Looking out at the pews was a scene as common and predictable as the sun going down behind the mountains and yet so moving. I saw sitting beside each person there the ghosts of generations past. I saw an encounter with the timeless.

As a Christian, every Sunday—in fact, every day, you are given many glimpses through the window of this life. Let your actions and words point those around you to that same glorious vista of what lies beyond, just as others did for you. Jesus' voice is calling. Teach others to recognize their Shepherd's voice and find peace in it, just as those who brought you to worship God did. Your life carries forward the past as it points with anticipation towards the future. Through Christ, you live in the past, present, and future, while transcending them all by your bond with the eternal, with Christ. You live at the crossroads of the eternal!

Study Questions

1. Comment on Bavinck's definition of the essences of a human being.
2. How can we transcend our physical and sensual existence?
3. Why are we often moved by common, yet timeless experiences?

Bibliography

Acton, Lord. "AZQuotes.com," http://www.azquotes.com/quote/1486.
Adams, John. "AZQuotes.com," http://www.azquotes.com/quote/1936.
Administrative Committee PCA, "PCA statistics: Five-year summary," www.pcaac.org.
Alinsky, Saul. *Rules for Radicals*. New York: Vintage, 1971.
Allen, Charlotte. "From little ACORNs, big scandals grow." *The Weekly Standard* November 3 (2008). www.weeklystandard.com.
Arendt, Hannah. *The Origins of Totalitarianism*. New York: Schocken, 2004.
Arnn, Larry P. "Time to give up, or time to fight on?" *Imprimis* 41 (December 2012).
Bavinck, Herman. *Reformed Dogmatics, Vol. 4: Holy Spirit, Church and New Creation*. Edited by John Bolt. Translated by John Vriend. New York: Baker Academic, 2008.
Berkhof, Louis. *Systematic Theology*. Grand Rapids: Eerdmans, 1996.
Bezmenov, Yuri. "Yuri Bezmenov: Deception Was My Job (Complete)." YouTube interview series with G. Edward Griffin, 1984.
Bonhoeffer, Dietrich. *The Cost of Discipleship*. New York: Simon and Schuster, 1959.
Boyle, Robert. "AZQuotes.com," http://www.azquotes.com/quote/587232.
Bradford, James T. "Report of the General Secretary," www.ag.org.
Callaway, Timothy Walton. *Callaway Baptist Preachers: 1789-1953*. LaGrange: Fuller E. Callaway Foundation, 1953.
Carr, Karen L. *The Banalization of Nihilism*. Albany: The State University of New York Press, 1992.
The Center for Research, Analytics and Data, "Statistical Profile, Fall 2014," uccfiles.com.
Chamblin, Knox. *Paul and the Self*. Eugene: Wipf & Stock, 1993.
Chesterton, G.K. *Heretics*. New York: Barnes & Noble, 2007.
Cialdini, Robert B. *Influence: Science and Practice, 4th ed.* Boston: Allyn and Bacon, 2001.
Covey, Steven J. *The 7 Habits of Highly Effective People*. New York: Simon and Schuster, 1989.

BIBLIOGRAPHY

DeCarlo, Neil. *Lean Six Sigma*. Indianapolis: Alpha, 2007.

de Chardin, Pierre Teilhard. "AZQuotes.com," http://www.azquotes.com/quote/53365.

Donne, John. "'Meditation 17', Devotions Upon Emergent Occasions." www.famousliteraryworks.com.

Dostoyevsky, Fydor. *The Brothers Karamazov*. New York: Penguin Classics, 2003.

Ellul, Jacques. *Propaganda: The Formation of Men's Attitudes*. New York: Vintage, 1965.

Enriquez, Juan. *As the Future Catches You*. New York: Crown Business, 2001.

Fernandez, Ignacio. *Felicidad Organizacional*. Santiago: B De Books, 2015.

Fettke, Tom. *The Hymnal for Worship & Celebration*. Waco: Word Music, 1986.

Foxe, John. *Foxe's Book of Martyrs*. Edited by W. Grinton Berry. Grand Rapids: Spire, 1998.

Frame, John. *Systematic Theology*. Phillipsburg: P&R, 2013.

Green, Erica L., Scott Calvert and Luke Broadwater, "Painful Lessons: Run-ins with students take toll on teachers, city finances." www.data.baltimoresun.com.

Greer, Scott. "D'Souza declares a strong connection between Hillary and Obama: It's Alinsky," *The Daily Caller* July 6 (2014) www.dailycaller.com.

Hamilton, Victor P. *The Book of Genesis: Chapters 1-17*. Grand Rapids: Eerdmans, 1990.

Hayden, Michael Edison, "4 officers shot within 24 hours amid violent year for police." www.abcnewsgo.com.

Hersey, Paul and Kenneth H. Blanchard, *Management of Organizational Behavior, 6th ed*. Englewood Heights: Prentice-Hall, 1993.

Holt, Jim. "Science Resurrects God," *The Wall Street Journal* (December 24, 1997).

Isaacson, Walter. *Steve Jobs*. New York: Simon & Schuster, 2011.

Jammer, Max. *Einstein and Religion: Physics and Theology*. Princeton: Princeton University Press, 2002.

Kinkaid, Paula R. "PCUSA continues membership decline - 92,433 members gone in 2014," www.layman.org

Koukl, Gregory. *Tactics: A Game Plan for Discussing Christian Convictions*. Grand Rapids: Zondervan, 2009.

Kreeft, Peter. *Christianity for Modern Pagans: Pascal's Pensees*. San Francisco: Ignatius, 1992.

———. *Making Choices*. Ann Arbor: Servant, 1990.

Kubler-Ross, Elizabeth. *On Death and Dying*. New York: Macmillan, 1969.

Kuebler, Brian, "Student on teacher assaults on rise." www.abc2news.com.

Lewis, C.S. *The Inspirational Writings of C.S. Lewis: Surprised By Joy, Reflections on the Psalms, The Four Loves, The Business of Heaven*. New York: Inspirational, 1986.

———. *The Problem of Pain*. New York: HarperSanFrancisco, 1996.

———. *The Screwtape Letters*. New York: HarperSanFrancisco, 1996.

Bibliography

McNeill, John T. *Calvin: Institutes of the Christian Religion*, Vol. 1. Louisville: Westminster John Knox, 1960.

Mendel, Gregor. *Experiments in Plant Hybridisation*. Cambridge: Harvard University Press, 1965.

Metaxas, Eric. *Bonhoeffer*. Nashville: Thomas Nelson, 2010.

Mueller, Benjamin and Al Baker, "Police officer is 'murdered for her uniform' in the Bronx." www.nytimes.com.

Newton, Isaac. "AZQuotes.com," http://www.azquotes.com/quote/575505.

Noyes, Rich. "*Clinton's an honest man.*" *News Flash* 3 (2005). www.mrctv.org.

Palmer, Donald. *Looking at Philosophy, 4th ed.* New York: McGraw-Hill, 2006.

Pascal, Blaise. "AZQuotes.com," http://www.azquotes.com/quote/225750.

Pietrusza, David ed. *Silent Cal's Almanac: The Homespun Wit and Wisdom of Vermont's Calvin Coolidge.* www.createspace.com, 2008.

Pipes, Richard. "Lenin's Gulag." *International Journal of Political Science and Development* 2 (2014) 140-146.

Polanyi, Michael. *Personal Knowledge*. Chicago: University of Chicago Press, 1962.

Ray, Dixy Lee and Lou Guzzo. *Environmental Overkill: Whatever Happened to Common Sense?* New York: Perennial, 1993.

Rummel, Rudolph J. *Death By Government*. New Brunswick: Transaction, 1994.

Russell, Bertrand. *The Impact of Science on Society*. New York: Simon & Schuster, 1953.

Ryken, Leland. *Worldly Saints*. Grand Rapids: Zondervan, 1986.

Schaeffer, Francis A. *Escape from Reason*. Downers Grove: IVP, 2006.

Schuman, Tomas. "Tomas Schuman (Yuri Bezmenov) L.A. 1983," YouTube.

Scott, Drusilla. *Everyman Revived: The Common Sense of Michael Polanyi*. Grand Rapids: Eerdmans, 1985.

Sebastian, Sharon. "Obama taught 'Destroy middle class.'" *Canada Free Press* October 12 (2012). www.canadafreepress.com.

Shakespeare, William. *The Complete Works of William Shakespeare. (Macbeth)*. New York: Avenel, 1975.

Solzhenitsyn, Aleksandr I. *The Gulag Archipelago, Vol. 1*, New York: Harper & Row, 1973.

———. *The Gulag Archipelago, Vol. 2*, New York: Harper & Row, 1975.

Sperry, Paul. "How Obama is bankrolling a nonstop protest against invented outrage." *New York Post* November 14 (2015). www.nypost.com.

Spielvogel, Jackson J. *Western Civilization, 6th ed.* Belmont: Thomson/Wadsworth, 2006.

Stark, Rodney. *The Victory of Reason*. New York: Random House, 2005.

Tackett, Del. "Veritology, What is Truth?" *The Truth Project Lesson 1* (2006) www.thetruthproject.org.

Taylor, Jr., Joseph Hooton. "AZQuotes.com," http://www.azquotes.com/quote/587231.

TenBoom, Corrie, John Sherrill and Elizabeth Sherrill. *The Hiding Place*. New York: Bantam, 1974.

BIBLIOGRAPHY

Vadum, Matthew. "Is ACORN violent unrest in Ferguson?" *The American Thinker* October 22 (2014). www.americanthinker.com.

Veith, Gene. *Postmodern Times*. Wheaton: Crossway, 1994.

Walton, Jeffrey. "Episcopalians continue bleeding members, attendance at alarming rate." https://juicyecumenism.com.

Webster, Noah. *An American Dictionary of the English Language, Revised edition* New York: Harper & Brothers, 1844.

Wendell Cox Consultancy, "Trends in Large US Church Membership from 1960," www.demographia.com.

Westminster Divines, *Westminster Confession of Faith*. Glasgow: Free Presbyterian Publications, 2001.

Woodward, Chris. "United Methodist decline due to liberal theology takeover," www.onenewsnow.com.

Yancey, Phillip. *Where Is God When It Hurts?* Grand Rapids: Zondervan, 1990.

Zacharias, Ravi. *Can Man Live Without God?* Nashville: W Publishing, 1994.

———. *The Real Face of Atheism*. Grand Rapids: Baker, 2004.

———. *Recapture the Wonder*. Brentwood: Integrity, 2003.

Subject Index

60 Minutes, 44

Abednego, 111
Abraham, 30
Adam, 19, 86
America, 23
American exceptionalism, 36
Ammonite, 67
Assemblies of God, 65
Audacity of Hope, 44

Bible, 5
Big bang, 19
Buddhism, 119

Captive, 66-67
Chinese communists, 75
Circles of Living, 48, 49
Committee of Public Safety, 37
Communist, 40
Communist Party of China, 39
Concentration Camps, 78-80, 109
Constitution, 23
Crisis, 73

Daniel, 108
David, 9
Death by Government, 38-40
Declaration of Independence, 23, 36
Declaration of the rights of man, 36, 37
Deconstructionism, 73
Democide, 39

Demoralization 73, 77
Destabilization, 73-74
Discipleship, 28
Dying to self, 24

Elijah, 106
Elisha, 82, 83
EPA, 45
Episcopal, 64
Escape from Reason, xi
Eve, 19

Facebook, 74
Faith, 91
Fall of man, 19, 86
Fallacy of the Righteous Average, 51-53
Father of Lies, 41
Founding Fathers, 38
French Revolution, 36, 38

General Revelation, 3, 5
God's megaphone, 95
Good Shepherd, 123
Google, 74
Gospel, Prosperity, 57
Gospel, Social Justice, 57
Grace, 4-5, 55
Grace, Cheap, 24, 55-57
Grace, Costly, 55, 56
Grace, Despised, 55, 58
Gravity, 1
Gulag, 47

Subject Index

Happiness, 85
Heidelberg Catechism, 104
Holocaust, 70
Holy of Holies, 90
Humpty Dumpty, 119

Ideology of Change, 75
Industrial Areas Foundation, 72
Institutes of the Christian Religion, 94
Isaac, 30

James, 25
Jefferson Memorial, 37
Jews, 109
Joseph, 108, 111
Judah, 108
Judge/judgment/judgementalism, 65-66

KGB, 73, 77

Lazarus, 25
Living Hope, 99
Lucifer, 72

Macbeth, 70-71
Marriage, 28
Marxism, 40
Marxist, 67
McGuffey reader, 18
Meshach, 111
Methodist, 64
Miracle, 2
Molech, 67

Natural law, 2
Nature, 2, 4-5
Nazi, 19
Nebuchadnezzar, 108
New Age, 87-88
Nihilism, 72
Nobel prize, 19
Normalization, 73, 77

Obedience, 26-30
Opiate of the masses, 86
Optimist, 86

Paganism, 119
Paul, 107-108
Peace, 85, 89, 91
Peniel, xv
Pentecostal, 65
Persecution, 63
Perseverance, 98
Peter, 28-29
Pharaoh, 108
Pilgrims, 23
Polecat, 11
Pontius Pilate, 44, 46
Postmodern Times, 72, 74
Postmodernism, 70, 74, 77, 81
Presbyterian, 64-65
Propaganda, 14
Protestant Reformers, 5
Puritan, 8, 23
Purposer, xiv

Radio, 2
Ravensbruk, 109
Recapture the Wonder, 89
Reformed Theological Seminary, 94
Reign of Terror, 37
Rules for Radicals, 72

Satan, 20, 72
Screwtape, 25, 67
Screwtape Letters, 49, 50
Senses, 83
Sermon on the Mount, 25
Shadrach, 111
Silas, 107-108
Social justice, 25
Special Revelation, 3, 5, 6
SS, 71, 79
Suffering, 93

The Hiding Place, 109
Thomas, 12
Totalitarian/Totalitarianism, 70, 74, 77-79
Tree of knowledge of good and evil, 19
Trinitarian, 94, 95

Subject Index

Triperspectivalism, 118
Turkey, 11
United Church of Christ, 64
Virtuousness, 25
Webster's Dictionary, 53
Wonder/Wonderful, 88, 90, 91
Word of God, 5
World War II, 8
Worldview, 2, 3
Wormwood, 67

Name Index

Acton, Lord John, 39
Adams, John, 23, 38
Alinsky, Saul, 72, 75
Aquinas, Thomas, 96
Arendt, Hannah, 70-71, 74, 76-79
Asbury, Francis, 37
Augustine, Saint, 96

Bavinck, Herman, 116, 118
Berkhof, Louis, 5, 55
Bezmenov, Yuri, 73, 77
Bonhoeffer, Dietrich, 22-32, 55-58
Boyle, Robert, 18
Bunyan, John, 96

Calvin, John, 85, 94, 97
Carr, Karen, 72
Chamblin, Knox, 94, 106
Chesterton, G.K., 102, 121-122
Cialdini, Robert B., 11
Clinton, Hillary, 72
Coolidge, Calvin, 37
Covey, Steven, 13

Darwin, Charles, 17
De Chardin, Pierre Teilhard, 115
DeCarlo, Neil, 8
Donne, John, 93, 96
Dostoyevski, Fyodor, 101

Einstein, Albert, 16, 19
Ellul, Jacques, 14
Emanuel, Rahm, 73
Enriquez, Juan, 51

Familia, Miosotis, 34
Fernandez, Ignacio, 85-86
Frame, John, 118, 121

Goebbels, Joseph, 19

Hamilton, Victor, 118-119
Himmler, Heinrich, 50, 71
Hitler, Adolf, 19, 71

Isaacson, Walter, 9

Jobs, Steve, 9

Koukel, Greg, 49
Kreeft, Peter, 100

Lenin, Vladimir, 46, 67, 86
Lewis, C.S., 23, 49-50, 67, 80, 95
Luther, Martin, 96, 97

Marx, Karl, 45
Mendel, Gregor, 19

Newton, Isaac, 19

O'Reilly, Bill, 44
Obama, Barack, 44, 71, 75-76

Pascal, Blaise, 6, 90
Polanyi, Michael, 16

Rather, Dan, 44
Rummel, R.J., 38
Russell, Bertrand, 74
Ryken, Leland, 8

Sarte, Jean-Paul, 44-45, 58-59
Schuman, Tomas, 73

Name Index

Scott, Drusilla, 16
Schaeffer, Francis, xi, 4
Shakespeare, William, 70
Sibbison, Jim, 45
Solzhenitsyn, Aleksandr, 45, 62-63, 98
Stalin, Joseph, 39, 46
Stark, Rodney, 17

Tackett, Del, 2
Taylor, Jr., Joseph H., 19
Ten Boom, Corrie, 109-110
Tse-Tung, Mao, 75

van Eck, Jan, 4
Veith, Gene, 72, 74, 76, 77

Watson, Paul, 45
Weinstein, Harvey, 72

Yancey, Philip, 96, 97

Zacharias, Ravi, 69-70, 89-90, 93, 96, 101

Scripture Index

GENESIS

2:16-17	20
2:16-17	90
3:1	20
3:4-5	20
3:5	36
3:15	19
17:23	30
22:1-14	30
32:22-32	xv
50:20	108, 111

NUMBERS

23:19	41, 52

DEUTERONOMY

8:11-20	22

JUDGES

17:6	27
21:25	35, 72

1 SAMUEL

8:4-5	73
8:7	73

2 SAMUEL

7:18	9

1 KINGS

19:1-9	106
19:12	9-10

2 KINGS

6:8, 14-17	82
6:14-17	117

JOB

8:13	76
42:5-6	99

SCRIPTURE INDEX

PSALMS

11:3	80
19:1	1, 3
23:4	32, 80
31:5	52
34:1	107
19:1-2	21
119:96	82, 89

PROVERBS

1:7	11, 18
18:22	16
25:24	15
27:6	15
27:17	94
27:19	15
31:10-11	15

ECCLESIASTES

4:9-10	16

ISAIAH

6:8	21
9:6	88
59:14-15	80
59:16	69
61:1	68
64:8	9

JEREMIAH

32:35	67

EZEKIEL

18:20	118

DANIEL

3:15	111
3:16-18	112

JONAH

1:1-3	106

MATTHEW

4:9	64
5-7	25
5:21-22	25
6:21	91
6:25, 28, 30	119
7:1-5	66
13:3-9	24
13:45-46	56
16:16	29
19:16-22	29-30
19:17	68
19:24	24
22:2-14	120
23:1-7	60
23:27-28	60
25:23	8
26:11	26
26:49	41
28:18	34, 42

MARK

14:21	113

LUKE

4:6-7	86
4:18	68
12:6	8
12:57	66
16:19-31	25

SCRIPTURE INDEX

JOHN

1:12	91
3:16-18	6
3:19	3-4
4:24	81
7:24	66
8:32	81
8:42-47	70
8:44	41
10:1-4	123
10:7-9	123
10:9	91
13:12-17	56
13:27	113
14:6	18, 44, 52, 80-81, 119
14:16-17	53
14:18	52-53
15:15-21	28-29
16:20, 23	97
16:13	53
17:15	24, 63
17:17	53
18:37	52, 66
18:38	44, 46
21:18	31
21:25	12

ACTS

16:16-34	107

ROMANS

1:18-20	3, 20
1:25	41, 52
3:10	42, 87
5:8	95, 113
6:1-2	57
6:3-6	113
6:20-22	41
7:15-25	27
8:17-21	98
8:28	95, 107, 111, 119
10:9	42
15:13	81, 88

1 CORINTHIANS

2:9	85
2:9-14	116-117
3:11	38
11:11	15
11:23-24	112
11:23-26	120
11:25-26	113
15:49	115

2 CORINTHIANS

4:6	85
4:17-18	102
7:4	100
12:9-10	98, 102
13:8	53

GALATIANS

2:15-16	68
2:20	27
3:1-3	54

EPHESIANS

1:4-10	9
4:4-6	81
5:19-20	107
5:25, 28, 33	16
6:14-17	53, 81

PHILIPPIANS

3:8	102
3:10-11	97
3:29	102
4:6	107
4:7	88

COLOSSIANS

1:24	102
2:8	67
3:17	107

1 THESSALONIANS

5:18	105, 107

2 THESSALONIANS

2:10-13	81

2 TIMOTHY

3:16	21

TITUS

2:11	55

HEBREWS

3:7	7
6:18	41, 52
11:1	112
11:3	21
11:11	21
11:13-16	112
11:36-40	112
13:2	120
13:15	107

JAMES

1:2-4	98
2:26	20-21, 25-26

1 PETER

1:6-7	98
3:7	16
4:13	102
5:8	67

1 JOHN

2:21	41
4:1	65
4:1-6	68

JUDE

10-13	7

REVELATION

7:17	95, 122
19:7-9	120

www.ingramcontent.com/pod-product-compliance
Lightning Source LLC
Chambersburg PA
CBHW050825160426
43192CB00010B/1904